Max Pemberton

Queen of the jesters

And her strange adventures in old Paris

Max Pemberton

Queen of the jesters

And her strange adventures in old Paris

ISBN/EAN: 9783741110696

Manufactured in Europe, USA, Canada, Australia, Japa

Cover: Foto ©Andreas Hilbeck / pixelio.de

Manufactured and distributed by brebook publishing software (www.brebook.com)

Max Pemberton

Queen of the jesters

A LOW WARNING ROAR THE BEAST SPRANG.

Queen of the Jesters

And Her Strange Adventures in Old Paris

By
Max Pemberton

Author of "Christine of the Hills"
"A Puritan's Wife," etc.

New York
Dodd, Mead and Company
1897

AUTHOR'S NOTE

THE adventures set out in these pages are taken from certain episodes in the life of Corinne de Montesson, who was long a famous figure in the Paris of Louis XV. Disdaining alike the salons of the great, where her wit would have given her a distinguished place, and the galleries of Versailles, where her indisputable beauty would have commanded a royal welcome, Mademoiselle de Montesson established herself in an old house in Rue St. Paul, and there, surrounded by a little band of wits, scientists, and adventurers, she made it her ambition to become acquainted with the dens of the city. To which end, she practised a generous charity, and rescued more than one notorious rogue from the gibbet. While the lower classes looked upon her now as a worker of miracles, now as a witch, the Court was greedy to hear of those exploits by which her name has come down to us. She had the privilege of entertaining the King on more than one occasion, and enjoyed to the end his support against the Lieutenant of Police, who bewailed her authority over the vagabonds of the

AUTHOR'S NOTE

city; and against her guardian, the Abbé Morellet, who demanded that she should be sent to a convent of Benedictine nuns. Sufficient to record that her influence was a continuing power in Paris until the year 1779, and that she died at the age of sixty-four years in her château at Fontainebleau.

CONTENTS

Chapter		Page
I.	The Hunger of Ferdinand Dauberval	1
II.	The Liberty of the Little Red Man	43
III.	A Prison of Swords	83
IV.	At the House of the Scarlet Witch	123
V.	The Purple Glass	165
VI.	The Kingdom of Bourgorieau	203
VII.	The Devil's Bowl and the Strange Affair at Fontenay	223
VIII.	Yerut the Dwarf	259

THE HUNGER OF FERDINAND DAUBERVAL

Queen of the Jesters

I

THE HUNGER OF FERDINAND DAUBERVAL

It wanted about an hour to sunset when Ferdinand Dauberval, sick with hunger and fatigue, passed through the Porte St. Denis and asked of the guard there the way to the Rue St. Paul.

"I am from Avranches, monsieur," said he, "and though you may not think it from my appearance, this is the first time that I have set eyes upon the city of Paris."

The guard thus addressed was a tall, good-humoured fellow, mounted upon a great black horse. He looked down, half in pity, half in amusement, at the dust-begrimed young man, who now clung to his stirrup-leather, if possible to rest his weary legs for a moment.

"*Sang bleu!*" said the guard. "If I took note of your appearance, my friend, I should think a good many things. You are from Avranches, you say? Then what have you to do in the Rue St. Paul?"

"That is my business," replied Dauberval, sulkily; but correcting himself in a moment, he added, "though I don't know why I should not tell you. I seek Mademoiselle de Montesson at the Hôtel Beautreillis. You know her house?"

The guard answered with a merry sneer.

"Oh," cried he, "I should know that house pretty well — all the beggars in Paris go there. Follow the first blind man from the Quinze-Vingts Infirmary and he will lead you to the door like a dog at the end of a string."

Dauberval, weak as he was, flushed with anger at the insult.

"Do you think that I ask alms?" he exclaimed.

"I am sure of it," answered the guard, smiling maliciously; "*Dame!* you look as though you had not seen a crown for a twelvemonth. I should advise you to make haste. They close the gate at curfew, and then there is no more bread nor hot bean soup. You would not like to hear that, eh?"

Dauberval swore a big oath.

"If I had you upon the stones," he snarled, "I would knock some sense into your silly head. Do you not see to whom you are talking? Oh, this Paris is a pretty place for a gentleman!"

THE HUNGER OF DAUBERVAL

He could have cried with his vexation, for pride, and pride alone, had brought him to the capital. It was true that his boots were in holes, while his clothes were so covered with the dust that their quality was not to be discerned; but still he plumed himself that his bearing and his manner of speaking were such as became the son of the advocate of Avranches, and it was galling to the point of madness that the first Parisian he met should talk to him as one would talk to a leper upon the steps of a parish church.

"To-morrow," cried he, shaking his fist at the little group of idlers who had gathered about the horseman, — "to-morrow, I will return with my friends."

"Hark to that," roared a bellman, who was one of the first to come up, "the dusty gentleman has friends. He will return with them to-morrow. Let the Grand Chamberlain be informed, and the pages provided. Where is his excellency's horse?"

"Do we know to whom we are talking?" chimed in a merry cooper, who stood with his hoops flung over his shoulder, — "well, it's my belief that we talk to our Lord the Pope — "

"Or to the Captain of the Gate," suggested a laughing hussy.

"Or to both," said a rat-catcher.

Dauberval answered them with a word hissed out between his teeth. If he had not been so weak from hunger and fatigue, he would have run away from them, but as it was, he only walked on down the Rue St. Denis, cursing the day which had carried him to Paris; and that other day when he staked his last crown on a throw of the dice at Couches — and had lost it. Never had he thought that he, whose younger brother was high in the service of the Grand Equerry, would come to look with hungry eyes upon the bread which the very beggars ate, — much less that he himself would be mistaken for a beggar.

"Pah!" he muttered, while he fought the phantoms of hunger who seemed to dance up from the dirty gutters bearing loaves of sweet white bread in their hands, "why should I despair? The Rue St. Paul cannot be far from here, and Mademoiselle Corinne will know how to cure my troubles. Did she not find a place for Armand, my brother — and what a place! It is true that he has told her lies about me — but I shall answer them. And she will believe me. A pretty woman always believes a man when he is young and —"

He added in his heart " good-looking;" although it did occur to him that he would need a great deal of brushing and mending before he could appear without shame in Mademoiselle Corinne's pres-

THE HUNGER OF DAUBERVAL

ence. He consoled himself, however, with the thought that her lacqueys would do this for him while their mistress was causing a good hot dinner to be prepared; and so keen was his imagination that the warmth of the food he awaited seemed already to fill his body with a delicious glow of heat. He began, in his fancy, to smell the pungent odour of spices; he said that he would arrive in the Rue St. Paul about the hour of supper, and that a fat capon might possibly be set before him. The horrible overpowering nausea, which was the result of his hunger, almost left him in the presence of these suggestions. He moved his mouth with the action of a man eating heartily, and a momentary return of his bodily strength enabled him to run straight on until he came out upon the Quai de l'Hôtel de Ville, and beheld the spires of Notre Dame stand up before him.

Paris was beginning to wake to the pleasures of her night then; and although it was early in the month of April in the year 1760, many people were abroad in the streets, sitting before the doors of their houses, or returning from their walk upon the ramparts. The great river itself was alive with boats; some filled by noisy students who played upon horns and drums; others with more orderly citizens bound for the wine-gardens and taverns of Passy. Dauberval stood a minute upon the quay to let the cool breeze play upon his burning face, and to watch the many strange figures and the many strange sights about him. He saw that he had never thought Paris could be so big. What a maze of threatening, cramped, yet picturesque houses was that upon the great island before him! How the cathedral dominated it all. Were there ever such fine fellows as these bucks and gallants on their way to dance with the butter-girls at the Quai de Gesvreo! Did any one ever hear such gibberish as these German mountebanks were talking! How the professional psalm-singers drawled! And there was a puppet-show too; and an acrobat from Italy, and a peoples' letter-writer, and a hundred others; all merry, and busy, and withal good-humoured, because the day was done with and the lights had begun to twinkle in the city.

Dauberval would have been content at any other time to have spent a day upon this busy quay, but the hunger tearing at his vitals quickly made him remember his errand. He asked of a petty wench who was selling cocoa — " two goes for a liard " — the way to the Rue St. Paul, and she answered him with a saucy laugh.

"*Ventrebleu!*" she cried, "that you should be so blind — yonder it stands as close to your feet as a fool's cap to his head. Oh, all the world can see where you come from."

THE HUNGER OF DAUBERVAL

"And the Hôtel Beautreillis?" asked Dauberval, too weak to argue with her.

"At the corner past the Rue Charlemagne. Stop under the great bronze lamp and tell the concierge that you are a simple young man from the country. He will give you five sous to buy your supper with, and I will give you a drink of cocoa for nothing."

She held out her can to him, and he took a little sup of the cocoa; but so great was his impatience to get to Mademoiselle Corinne's house that he would not wait for the boiling stuff to cool, but ran on when he had gulped down a few drops of it. A minute later, he found himself under the shadow of the great walls of the Hôtel Beautreillis; and he saw the bronze lamp which the hussy had named. But it was unlighted, and the forbidding iron-sheathed door in the quaint Norman tower at the corner of the street offered to him a heart-breaking welcome. How, he asked, if the pretty philanthropist whom he had walked all the way from Avranches to see, were at her country house near Gros Bois? His brain went whirling round at the thought! He prayed to God — and it was many a year since a prayer had come to his lips — that his burden of suffering might not have this new evil added to it.

The Rue St. Paul was almost deserted at that

hour. Long black shadows were stealing over the muddy flags of the wretched street. A few flickering lanterns cast a dull gleam of yellow light upon the dirty water of the open gutter. In the great house itself a dreadful silence reigned. Not a lamp shone in any of the narrow windows; not a footfall was to be heard in any of the courts. Dauberval beat with his fists upon the heavy oaken door, but he might as well have struck at the wall of the Bastille. No one answered to his puny knocking. He picked up a flag from the gutter and hurled it at the iron armour of the gate, but got for his pains only the weird echoes which went booming from cloister to cloister, and from tower to tower. And his hunger was now irresistible, horrible. His whole body seemed to be wasting away as he stood.

"Oh, *mon Dieu!*" he wailed, wringing his hands, and sobbing for very weakness, "have pity, have pity — one little drink of milk, oh, for Christ's sake."

He thought surely that he was dying; and it was cruel, he said, that he must perish of hunger at the very gate of his fortunes. The possibility that pretty Mademoiselle Corinne, who had done so much for his younger brother, Armand, might be at her château near Gros Bois, had not come into his reckoning until that moment. Never

THE HUNGER OF DAUBERVAL

before in all his life had he known the meaning of hunger. He sat upon the stone steps before the unyielding door, and it seemed to him that a hundred demons were dancing round him, each bearing a tempting dish or a goblet of rich red wine. He beat them off with his fists, and others arose to caress him with visions of splendid feasts and tables groaning. His greedy eyes searched the gutters in the vain hope that an untrodden crust might lie there. He dipped his hands in the water of a shining puddle and bathed his burning forehead; but it only burned the more. He muttered a new prayer; and it was this — that his death might come quickly, and that he might suffer such agony no longer. And this was a prayer to which an answer was vouchsafed — but not such an answer as he had looked for.

Truth to tell, it all came upon him very suddenly. He had sunk down upon the step then, and his cheek was resting upon a slab of marble. Pain had begun to give way to unconsciousness; the turbid dreams to utter darkness of the mind. But from such a state of trance he awoke presently to find that the rays of a lantern were flashing in his eyes, and that a man dressed from head to foot in black had gripped him firmly by the arm. He had heard strange tales of the footpads of Paris; and his yawning imagination convinced him, for an awakening idea, that one such rogue sought to rob him. At any other time he would have laughed loudly at the notion; but now he was too weak to laugh — too weak almost to stand.

"*Pardieu!*" he snarled, "what the devil do you want with me? Can't you see — ?"

The man answered him with a word spoken to another at his elbow.

"Aubin," said he, "take the right arm of Monsieur Dauberval, and let Joseph bring another lantern."

Dauberval started up when he heard his name. The dazzling rays no longer blinded his eyes. He saw that the stranger's black vest was richly embroidered with silver, and that diamonds sparkled upon the hilt of his sword. Beyond this, the great door of the Hôtel Beautreillis was now wide open, and servants were busy in its courtyard. Dauberval, who had been ready to declare that the apparition was a new cheat of his fancy, doubted no longer. Mademoiselle Corinne was in Paris. What was more, she knew that he was hungering at her gates. Never did a man's fortune seem to be made so readily.

"Monsieur," said he to the unknown, as they passed the lodge of the concierge, and so entered the vast central courtyard, "you have my name!"

"Assuredly," said the other. "Your name is

Ferdinand Dauberval, and you are the son of the advocate of Avranches. Five days ago, you left your home to walk to this house — having first robbed your father of a hundred crowns, the last of which you lost over the dice at Couches two days ago. I speak rightly, monsieur?"

Dauberval stood still with his astonishment.

"*Ciel!*" he cried, "you insult me, monsieur?"

"Oh, not at all," replied the unknown. "You put a question to me, and I answer it. Is that an insult?"

"You say that I robbed? — " expostulated Dauberval.

"Come, come," said the other, a little severely. "I really cannot argue with you, Monsieur Dauberval. While we wait in this draughty courtyard, your supper is getting cold. Remember how hungry you are."

Dauberval, trembling with excitement, permitted himself to be led across the court and so to the smaller pavilion upon the left-hand side of it.

"I shall make up some tale," he thought, "and she will believe me. Meanwhile, there will be food to eat and wine to drink. *Dieu*, how I could drink a cup of Burgundy! It will be time after that to remember my misfortunes."

Like all rogues, he was easily elated. And the things which he saw about him were of a quality to satisfy any man. No sooner had he entered the pavilion than lacqueys came unbidden to brush his clothes and to bring a golden basin for his hands. While one fellow begged him to be seated and to remove his dirty shoes, another offered him a coat of velvet heavily laced with silver braid. Everything that greed of show and of wealth could prompt him to wish for was now thrust upon him unasked. Silk stockings took the place of his dusty woollen ones; the perfume of attar of roses exuded from the cooling water in which he washed the dust from his face; the lacqueys waited upon him with a homage which might have served a king. And this was the mystery of it all — that they did these things for one whom their mistress knew to be a thief.

Dauberval was too hungry at the first to debate upon such a nice problem. He did observe that the unknown man in black watched him with a curious smile — the smile of one who enjoyed some secret, but did not wish to share it. Yet this, he said, was the man's satisfaction at his new appearance. Indeed, the stranger told him so presently, when he rose to conduct him to his supper.

"*Ma foi*, Monsieur Dauberval," said he, " you will break some hearts in Paris. I never saw a coat sit so well upon a man. And you know how to carry it, too. Saint Denis, we must find you

THE HUNGER OF DAUBERVAL

a sword presently, when the perruquier has done with you. You can use a sword, I will wager?"

Dauberval, who was the greatest coward in Normandy, drew himself up and bowed at the compliment.

"Sir," said he, "if I were not so hungry —"

"Exactly, my friend. And since you are very hungry — come, supper is prepared for you."

He opened a door in the ante-chamber to which they had first come, and motioned the other to go forward. Dauberval could scarce suppress a cry of delight when he saw that a table was spread in an exquisitely furnished cabinet; and that other lacqueys waited to serve him with all those good things of which he had lately dreamed. Nay, he was not sure that he did not dream still, for this room, he said, must surely be one in which kings supped. Such divinely wrought candelabra, such a painted ceiling, such a profusion of wax tapers, so soft a carpet, were not to be looked for except at the palace of the Tuilleries or at Versailles. Dauberval declared that the owner of it all must be rich beyond any woman in Paris. "And," he said, "she means well to me or I should not be here."

This self-assurance brought him to the table in wondrous good spirits. Although he had suffered much from his hunger, he was not so far gone that eating would be a danger to him; and when a lacquey put a little bowl of soup before him, he drank it down in great gulps. The warmth of it seemed to fill his body to the very toes.

"Oh," he said, "how good it is — how good! Surely it is well to have suffered, monsieur, if one may —"

At this moment he turned round to find himself alone with the lacquey in the cabinet. The unknown had left him at the door; and Dauberval really was not sorry to be quit of his company.

"One can do nothing with a man," he thought; "and he is gone to tell pretty Mademoiselle Corinne that I am here. She will come to see me presently, and I shall persuade her that I am a very honest fellow. After that, she will find me some place in Paris, and I shall have lacqueys of my own, and wine like this Burgundy. Saint John, how it warms my heart! And I have yet the half of a bottle to drink! Oh, it was a great day that took me from Avranches to my fortune at the Hôtel Beautreillis!"

Hopes like these, with a hundred others, filled his brain, while he helped himself to a dish of artichokes fried in marmalade, and afterwards to the breast of a well-boiled capon. He was careful to eat sparingly of the food, remembering how long he had fasted; but of the wine he drank abun-

THE HUNGER OF DAUBERVAL

dantly. Nor did the lacqueys once speak to him while he ate. They might have been machines answering to some invisible wires. Dauberval, warmed with the Burgundy, began to assume lofty and patronising airs. He even attempted to enter into conversation with one of those who waited upon him.

"My good fellow," said he, " is your mistress in Paris?"

The man bowed, but that was all his answer. Dauberval, more than ever anxious to play the part of the fine gentleman, pushed his chair away from the table and leant back in it posingly.

"Have the goodness," he cried, " to inform Mademoiselle de Montesson that I crave a word with her so soon as it may please her to give me audience."

The lacquey bowed again, and left the room with his fellows. He was careful not to laugh until he had shut the door upon his mistress's guest; but then he laughed very heartily. Dauberval, meanwhile, was leaning back in his chair, and telling himself that this for a surety was the day of his life.

"She cannot mean to punish me for borrowing two hundred crowns of my father," he said to himself, " or she would not have treated me like this. No doubt she has heard some slander; but I shall correct all that. And then she will give me a place. Possibly it will be with the Grand Equerry, where my brother is; or should there be no vacancy there, I would even submit to serve for a while as page to his highness the Duke of Nevers. In any case she will make my fortunes. Who knows, she might even think me handsome, as the girls of Avranches did. And then — *pardieu!* — and then — "

To his utter confusion, a voice of singular sweetness answered his question, which he had intended for no other ears than his own.

"And then, Monsieur Dauberval?"

"*Diable!*" cried the man, as he sprang up from his chair and turned round to face the intruder. But the other words he would have spoken died away upon his lips; for there, standing behind him, with the merriest laugh possible upon her pretty face, was Mademoiselle Corinne. And so great was the shame of the fellow because his silly talk was overheard that he would have thanked God if the earth had opened and swallowed him up.

"Mademoiselle," he stammered, and he was sure that he had never seen a more exquisite vision than this of the owner of all these riches, — "mademoiselle, I do not — indeed."

"Oh," she said, laughing more than ever at his confusion, "but you did. And let me tell you, monsieur, that I think the girls of Avranches showed exceedingly good taste."

Dauberval, like most rogues, could bear himself well in ordinary circumstances before a woman. He had looked to find a grand dame, haughty, imperious, exacting; but now that Mademoiselle Corinne really stood before him, and he saw that she was an exceedingly beautiful girl, whose face wore the kindliest smile he had ever beheld, he took new courage and began to look up.

"Mademoiselle," he exclaimed, "you overheard me just now saying some very foolish things. I thought that I was alone or I should not have uttered them. I beg you to forgive me."

"Indeed, monsieur," she answered, still smiling, "I shall do nothing of the sort. You have yet to answer my question. Here am I agreeing with the young ladies you speak of, and dying to know what next — yet you tell me nothing. For shame, monsieur, to leave a lady ailing with her curiosity."

"Misfortune overtake me if I do any such thing," cried Dauberval, bowing gallantly, "yet, for the life of me, mademoiselle, I cannot remember what I was saying."

"Oh, but I remember it perfectly, Monsieur Dauberval," she answered; "you were saying 'and then —' I want to know what comes after 'and then' —"

QUEEN OF THE JESTERS

A quick thought passed like an inspiration through the man's mind.

"Mademoiselle," he cried, "you insist?"

"Certainly I do."

"Then I will tell you in a word. I was saying to myself as you came in that if I should be happy enough to merit your favor, you would find me some place in Paris."

He stood watching her keenly to see how his boldness would be repaid; but her immediate answer was only a command.

"Sit, *mon ami*," she said, "and then we will talk of things."

Dauberval took a chair and drew it near to the little couch upon which she was resting. He was so close to her now that he could count the diamonds which made a rope about her lovely neck. He said that he had never seen such surpassing loveliness of skin or face; never a woman worthy to sit at the feet of Corinne de Montesson. The very air about her was laden with the breath of roses. Her girlish face was like the face of one of the Madonnas which the great masters had painted. Her voice was like the note of a silver bell.

"You wish me to find you a place in Paris, Monsieur Dauberval," she said, when they were seated. "Well, that is already done —"

"What," cried Dauberval, forgetting himself in

his surprise, — at the same time he said to himself, "My fortune is made."

"Yes," she continued, "after making all inquiries about you, I am willing to take you into my service."

Dauberval's expectation became tremendous. "She knows nothing," he thought.

"You will consent, I am sure, monsieur," Corinne went on, "to do as my other servants have done, and to attain promotion by your diligence and fidelity. Yet I do not forget that you were educated by the curé of Avranches, and are a man of some learning. On that account, I have determined to overlook all that I might remember about you, and to make you an usher of the table."

Dauberval listened no more, but sprang from his chair. He was white with passion when he answered her.

"*Dieu!* mademoiselle," he cried, "would you make a lacquey of me?"

"Exactly," she replied, without so much as noticing his temper; "an usher of my table to begin with, and after that clerk to my household, if your service in the first employment warrants it. It is even possible, should you seek by the future to blot out the sins of your past, that I may remember you as the brother of Armand

Dauberval — whom you drove from his home after accusing him falsely of a robbery."

"It is a lie!" stammered Dauberval, hoarse with his anger. "I am the victim of —"

Corinne de Montesson rose from her seat, and touched a gong at her side.

"Monsieur," she said very quietly, "to-night you remain here as my guest. If you are willing to accept the post which I offer you, hold yourself ready to begin your work at ten o'clock to-morrow morning. But I warn you that should you speak to me again as you spoke just now, my servants shall flog you at the tail of a cart. You understand me?"

There was laughter in her eyes no longer, and her cheek was warmed with a red flush. Dauberval realised for the first time what a great gulf lay between them. His hopes had gone tumbling down already pell-mell, like stones into a pit. He was cowed, and he trembled with rage and disappointment.

"*Ciel!*" said he, wringing his hands, "that you should wish to make a lacquey of me! Oh, mademoiselle, have pity — you know what I have suffered."

"Say rather, that I remember what your brother suffered at your hands," she replied. "Indeed, Monsieur Dauberval, you reap that which you have sown. Have a care, then, to treasure in the future the seeds of honesty and of love. I wish you good-night, monsieur."

She retired with a gentle grace, a lacquey holding the door as she passed to her own apartments. Dauberval followed her with eyes in which the tears of shame and cowardice welled up plenteously. Her words had stung him like a whip; yet, he said, he could have forgotten them quickly enough had she not sought to put this insult upon him. But to make a lacquey of him! Better by far to have remained in Avranches, he thought, and to have extorted money from his father. There, at any rate, people did not forget that he was born a gentleman. But here, in this unpitying Paris — to make a menial of him, he who had dreamed that he was soon to have lacqueys of his own! Oh, it was not to be tolerated!

He had been pacing the room for some little time, gathering the threads of his anger, when the servant returned to tell him that his bed-chamber was prepared. He followed the fellow sullenly, determined already in his own heart that he would never submit to the proposed degradation. After all, he could still return to his home and say, "Father, I have sinned." It would be a terrible humiliation; but he preferred the thought of facing it to that of remaining in the Hôtel Beautreillis.

QUEEN OF THE JESTERS

As for his brother Armand — it would be no use to beg of him. Dauberval knew well enough that he had driven his brother from their home, caring nothing if he lived or died. How then should that brother pity him?

The lacquey, meanwhile, had conducted him down a long stone corridor; thence across a little garden, and through a second passage, which terminated in a small circular hall off which five doors opened. Dauberval scarce took notice of anything that he passed; but when the lacquey opened the third of the five doors and informed him that here was his bed-chamber, a new interest occupied him. None of Mademoiselle Corinne's reproaches seemed to fit in with the elegance of the room to which he had been conducted. It was a room for the king, he said for the second time, while the man lighted the candles in the gilt sconces and set a cup of wine upon the table. The great bed with the canopy of gold above it; the superb tapestries hung upon the wall; the many candelabra of solid silver; the luxurious carpet beneath his feet, — all these things should have been at Versailles, he thought, and not at the Hôtel Beautreillis. And it was maddening to him to remember that he was to enjoy such splendours for one night, and only for one night.

"To-morrow," he snarled, for the servant had

left him then, — "to-morrow they will make a lacquey of me! Oh, that shall never be! I swear it on the cross. She shall listen to me in the morning — I will go on my knees to her — I will humble myself — she will surely relent then. She must relent."

He repeated these words again and again, and they were still upon his lips when he climbed into the high bed and stretched himself luxuriously upon the downy cushions. The candle was out now, and the moon's beams flooded the room picturesquely, seeming to magnify its size and beauty. Indeed, the very splendours of the apartment awed the man. He lay for a long while unable to sleep, or to do anything but contemplate the things he would plan and say when morning came. When he had settled those to his satisfaction, and sleep still refused her friendship, he began to follow the path of the pale yellow rays and to observe the beauty of the things they touched with their caressing light. He remarked then for the first time a little picture of a Madonna hung near the wall by his bed; and when he had looked at this for some moments, he saw that it was the central piece of a shrine upon which there was a cross with a great diamond blazing in the centre of it. So beautiful were the lights which the jewel scattered, so large was it, that Dauberval asked himself why he had not seen it before. Then he sat up in bed the better to observe it, but lay down again quickly lest the thought which came to him so powerfully should remain and prevail.

"She must be very rich," he said, as he drew the clothes over his head and fought anew for sleep. "That diamond alone would keep a man in food and wine for life. She has many more like it, I am sure, and would never miss it. If a rogue were sleeping here, he would put that cross in his pocket and she would never know its loss. Besides, she is going to make a lacquey of me. Saint John — I could be even with her if I had the mind to!"

He lay for some moments trembling with the excitement of the thought. He knew that such a diamond as the one which lay within reach of his hand would enrich him for life. He had but to slip the cross into his pocket and to climb the wall of the garden through which he had passed to his room, and he need think of being a lacquey no more. What a revenge that would be, he said. And why did he owe her any mercy? She had shown him none. Nay, she had threatened to have him beaten at a cart's tail. "We shall see about that," he muttered — and then he sat up in bed again. The diamond shone now with a finer, richer lustre. All the loveliest hues seemed to be commingled, and to be poured out together from its sparkling wells of light. Dauberval had not dreamed that there was such a jewel in all the world. The sight of it was to him like a cup of wine to a drunkard. "Heaven!" he muttered, "it is a prince's ransom — and I am alone."

He was out of bed now, and his teeth were chattering with dread of his determination. While he said all the time that he was not going to steal the diamond, he knew perfectly well that he had made up his mind to do so. Quickly and with trembling hand he drew on his boots and his fine new coat. He opened his bedroom door, and found to his satisfaction that the little hall outside was in darkness and as silent as the grave. Everything drove him on to the crime which he declared that he would never commit, but which he was even then committing. Twice he touched the diamond, and drew back his hand as though it had been burned by fire.

"Coward," he cried, "coward, coward — to turn your back on a fortune which lies there before your eyes. Ten steps and you are in the garden; you leave Paris at dawn and set out for England — a little hiding by the way, perhaps, a little privation — and then, and then — !"

Visions of luxury, of ease, even of vice, passed before his burning eyes. A new hunger, the hunger of wealth, was upon him now. The agonies of the temptation were like the agonies of a burning fever. He stood rocking on his heels before the shrine, saying, "I will not, I will not." He covered his face with his hands, yet the lights from the sparkling jewel seemed to flash into his very brain. When at last he grasped the stone with trembling fingers, and thrust it deep down into his bosom, phantoms of the night gathered about him in his fancy and cried, "We see, we see."

With possession, the fever abated a little. He was in a cold sweat now; but his ideas were less confusing. When he opened his bedroom door to pass into the circular hall, he knew well enough what plan to follow. The garden, he was sure, lay not more than twenty yards from him. He had seen, while they had conducted him to his room, great trees growing against the walls of it, and he determined to climb this wall by their help and so to gain the street.

He opened his door, and stood for a moment to listen if there were any sound about the house. A little whisper of the wind sighing in the dome of the hall was the only answer to his silent question. Encouraged by the stillness, he stepped from his chamber and began to creep towards that door of the five through which he believed that he had passed to his bedroom. And here a difficulty which he had not foreseen suddenly presented itself and demanded consideration. The five doors in the hall were as alike as five drops of water. How if he opened the wrong one, and found himself, not in the garden, but in the bed-chamber of some lacquey or page? That, he declared, would mean the galleys at the least. And he blamed himself now that he had not tried the doors before leaving his bedroom. To be taken with the jewel in his possession were a folly indeed.

Dauberval was a cunning rogue at all times; but he did not know what forces of cunning and trickery were being pitted against him as he stood debating the puzzle of the doors. At the very moment when he thought he was alone, six pairs of eyes were watching him with interest and not a little amusement. True, there was a moment when he had an instinctive warning of peril hovering about him, and that was the moment when the door of the bedroom he had just quitted shut suddenly and the key grated ominously in the lock.

"*Mort Christ!*" he muttered, "my door has locked itself — I heard the key turn — what a thing to happen!"

There was no doubt about it at all. The door had shut and the key had turned. Dauberval stood like one petrified, pressing the jewel to his breast with both his hands, and telling himself that the wind had done the work. So unnerved was he that he did not lift a foot until minutes had passed and no other sound had come to break the whispers of the night. The vision of the galleys and the whip was ever before his eyes. When at length he moved again, it was this vision which gave him strength.

"Bah!" he said, "am I a woman to start at the fall of a pebble? If I stand here much longer I shall go to sleep, and a lacquey will find me at daybreak. Courage, then — a little courage and all is well."

The idea put new life into him. He tried the first of the doors, but it was locked; and the second, in like manner, refused to yield to his hand. Only when he came to the fourth door did he take heart and say that success was near to him. For that door opened readily at his touch; and when he had hesitated a moment lest it should lead him to a room and not to a passage, he pushed it back inch by inch that the little light in the hall might break the darkness which now blinded him. He would have given half he possessed to hold a lantern for a minute then, so dark was the place in which he found himself; but he knew that he could not work miracles, and so he nerved himself for a last effort and boldly passed the door. In the same instant, the place was flooded by a soft yellow light, and Mademoiselle Corinne stood face to face with him.

She was dressed in a loose gown of muslin, spotlessly white and unornamented, and she held a golden candlestick high above her head that the light might fall upon the face of the man. Dauberval, staggering with terror, observed that a small diamond cross glittered upon her white neck, and that a great Russian hound crouched by her side and pressed his nose into her hand. She had entered the little cabinet through a panel opening in the wall at a spot exactly opposite to the door which led the rogue to this trap; but she appeared to be quite alone, and to know the purpose of her coming.

"Well, Monsieur Dauberval," she cried, and there was merriment in her voice, — "well, Monsieur Dauberval, are you not pleased to see me?"

Deceived by her manner, the robber looked up. "She is alone," he thought, "and she is a woman." But he made no attempt to answer her, seeking rather to escape from the room into the hall behind him. And at this she laughed aloud.

"For a truth, you are a bold fellow," she continued, as the man backed towards the door, "and I am very glad that you did not die at my gate to-night. Have a care to your steps, I beg of you, Monsieur Dauberval, or you will be of little service to the galleys. Shall I summon a lacquey to carry your plunder? How unfortunate that you should awake me at the very moment you were robbing my house!"

Something in the tone of her voice, a note of scorn mingling with the chord of her laughter, compelled the man to stand. It occurred to him that he must deal with her before he left the room, or assuredly she would awake the house, and he would be taken in the gardens of it. He determined to play first upon her pity.

"Mademoiselle," he exclaimed, coming a little nearer to her, and speaking with an effort, "you are very cruel to me — I could not sleep — I wished to walk a little way in your gardens — do you think that I am a robber? God forbid — I swear it on the cross."

"On the cross which you carry at your breast, Monsieur Dauberval?"

"*Ciel!*" he gasped, drawing back again, "you know about that?"

"You hear that I do; and since I know about it my servants are now going to carry you to the Palais de Justice, where you will have leisure to regret that you did not become a lacquey."

She said this, and with the words she took up a padded stick and raised it as though to beat upon the gong by which she stood. For a moment,

THE HUNGER OF DAUBERVAL

however, she held her hand; and forgetting that she had laughed, she went on to remind the man of that which he had lost.

"When you came to my house to-night," she said, " I was content to forget the life you have lived and the crimes you have committed. For your brother's sake, I thought to give you one more opportunity of becoming that which you will never be — an honest man. To-morrow, had you submitted for a day to the test which I chose for you, I would have remembered again that you were the son of the advocate of Avranches. You will not ask me to do that now, Monsieur Dauberval?"

Dauberval listened to her with burning ears. He watched the upraised stick as he would have watched a tiger about to leap upon him. He knew that if the gong were struck, his hope of life would die away with the echoes of the note.

"Mademoiselle," he wailed, "for God's sake spare me — you will never regret it — I swear it on my knees — hear me — you will not summon your servants?"

He fell upon his knees before her and raised his hands in cowardly entreaty. But her answer was unpitying.

"Nay," she said, "I am about to summon my servants now."

"*Dieu!* mademoiselle," muttered the man, springing to his feet, "you shall do nothing of the sort." But to himself he said again — "She is a woman, and she is alone."

All the devils of evil were spurring him on now. He knew that it was his life or hers — the life of a helpless girl or of a man with one foot already upon the scaffold. And he was going to plead with her no more. When he rose from the floor, he told himself that he would kill her. The madness of his mood magnified and became uncontrollable. He raised his hand to strike her down, shutting his eyes that he might not see the exquisite beauty of her face.

"You shall not do it," he cried savagely. "By Heaven, I will prevent you."

"Indeed," she cried, stepping back quickly, "it is already done;" and even as she spoke the blows fell, — that of the man in the air, that of the woman upon the silver gong.

Dauberval had struck wildly; but he struck no second blow. He had said "She is alone;" but never was she less alone. The great dog at her side, who had curled himself up to sleep while his mistress had no need of him, awoke at the booming of the gong, and was at the throat of the man, even while he reeled back for a new attack. With a low warning roar, the beast sprang at the robber, and felled him as an ox is felled by a butcher's axe. Over and over upon the wooden floor the two rolled; the dog growling ferociously, the man imploring, screaming, fighting. Death seemed to breathe into his very face now. He had his arm across his throat, and the hound's fangs touched the bone of it. He struck the brute again and again with his clenched fist; and for every blow his whole body was shaken until his teeth gnashed like the teeth of a madman.

"Kill me, kill me," he screamed, "for God's sake!— oh, he is tearing me limb for limb! Heaven!— what suffering!"

He had rolled now almost to the door of the room, and there the hound drew back for a moment, hearing his mistress's voice. Dauberval, mad with fear and pain, scrambled to his feet and staggered out into the hall of the unyielding doors. A light was there now; and one of the five doors stood wide open before him; but he had no thought of asking how or for what reason. Dread of the dog drove him onward recklessly. "Anything, anything but that," he cried; and reeling, staggering, sobbing, he passed through the door and down the long passage to which it gave access. Whither he was going or to what end, he knew not nor cared to think. One idea dominated him to the exclusion of all others — it was the idea of flight

— flight to any refuge, even the refuge of the scaffold.

There was very little light in the corridor where he now found himself, and when he had run perhaps twenty yards he turned a sharp corner and was then in utter darkness. So black was it that he could not see the ground at his feet. He guided himself only by touching the wall with his fingers. It was a smooth wall, a panelled one, he saw at first; and though he knew that he might go tumbling headlong down a staircase, or crashing against a door at any step, so great was his terror that he ran heedlessly, believing ever to hear the patter of the hound's paws upon the ground behind him, even to feel his wet and frothing lips against his hand. And he was becoming exhausted now. Often he reeled against the wall and thought that he was fainting. Would he never come into the garden, he asked? He had been running for long minutes now, and still the dreadful wall guided him onward, onward. Once he paused, panting for his breath, but his ear told him plainly that the hound had followed him. There was no mistaking that haunting "pat, pat, pat," behind him. "God have mercy — he will tear me limb from limb," he cried, and so wailing he began to run again.

Dauberval was a man who had known few hardships in life; but just as the past two days had taught him what it is to hunger, so did this night of agony teach him the meaning both of fear and fatigue. He had not dreamed that a man could conceive so great a horror and loathing as this horror and loathing of the hound which now possessed him. As to his fatigue, there were no words to tell of that. His life seemed to exude from his body drop by drop. Every step was a torture to him. The tears ran down his face like rain; a spasm gripped his heart and seemed to hold it still; his legs were so weary that he could scarce lift them from the ground. And to his terror of the seen, the terror of the unseen was now added. He had run for the third part of an hour by this time; and still the terrible wall led him on. He began to say that fiends were cheating him — for how could the Hôtel Beautreillis possess a corridor down which a man might run for twenty minutes? That would carry him half across Paris. Under any other circumstances he would have tried to reason with the situation, but the ominous patter of the hound banished reason from his head. More than this, he heard the soft tread of other hounds now before him, now behind him. He shrieked aloud with his fear, and fled again like a madman.

There is an end to the endurance of terror and of the false strength which it inspires. Dauberval kept his legs to the ultimate moment, for he told himself that if he fell, the hounds would tear him as they would tear a deer. But at last pitying nature came to his aid. He remembered only that he stretched out his hands before him, staggering blindly into the darkness. Then, with a terrible cry, for he heard the dogs at his very feet, he fell senseless to the floor and lay like a dead man.

When he opened his eyes, hours had passed. The ghostly dawn light streaming through a lantern tower above him told him that day had broken; but he lay motionless for long minutes, unable to remember how he had come into the place where now he was, or why he slept upon a wooden floor. He was still very weak, and his limbs were cold and stiff and painful; his brain burnt, and would shape no story for him. When at last he began to remember the events of the dreadful night, he thought first of the diamond, and pressed his hands to his breast instinctively; but the jewel was gone; nor could he recollect how he had lost it. By and by he recalled the moment when he had left his bed-chamber; and that other moment when pretty Mademoiselle Corinne stood before him and he had struck her, and from that thought he passed to memory of the hound. So potent was this in terror, that it compelled him to stagger to his feet. Half awake as he was, the whole dread of the night came rushing back to him. He could hear the hound still — that he would swear; and even when he stood up and asked himself, "Where am I?" the haunting "pit, pat" still sang in his ears.

"Oh, *mon Dieu!*" he wailed, "have I lost my reason? Where am I? What do I hear? Oh, pity me, pity me!"

He looked all about him and could make nothing of his environment. He was in a great building, certainly, — a building which looked like a riding-school, and was in the shape of an oval. He observed clearly that a high wall ran round this building, and that he had been lying upon a wooden corridor which made a little platform beneath the wall. Dense as he was, it began to dawn upon him that he had been running round and round this corridor; and at this thought he trembled with passion.

"Heaven!" he cried, "that I should have run round and round like a horse which amuses the people — oh, what cruelty to play me such a trick — what cruelty — "

His distress was so great that he began to wring his hands and to pace the corridor distractedly. And he had been engaged in this employment for the space of a minute, when the second of his delusions was taken from him. For, suddenly, he came upon a little fountain built into the wall of the riding-school; and as he stood a minute to bathe his hands and forehead at it, it occurred to him that the music of it was familiar; and that its "drip, drip, drip" was just like the pat of a dog's paw upon the ground. "Holy Saints!" he cried with a sob, "that I should have run away from a basin of water. There is the patter of my hound. Oh, God! what a night of agony!"

A mocking laugh was the answer to his word of ultimate distress. He turned round to find himself in the presence of the man in black, who had met him at the gate yesterday; and he saw that a lacquey awaited the orders of the unknown.

At sunset that evening, Ferdinand Dauberval passed through the Porte St. Denis on his way to his father at Avranches.

"Halloa," cries the bellman, "here is the dusty gentleman who has friends. *Bon soir*, monsieur — was the king well when your excellency dined with him?"

"It is my belief that we talk to our Lord the Pope," exclaimed the cooper.

"Or to the Captain of the Gate," said the saucy wench.

"Or to both," shouted the rat-catcher.

But the mounted guard laughed heartily, and cried: —

"Good-day, little fire-eater! Did they give you

alms at the Hôtel Beautreillis. Saint John, what an honest face you have! Oh, it is plain that you are a loss to Paris!"

Dauberval stood for a moment to shake his fist at them. Then he passed the gate, and Paris knew him no more.

.

THE LIBERTY OF THE LITTLE RED MAN

II

THE LIBERTY OF THE LITTLE RED MAN

Coq le Roi, the highwayman, started up in his bed when the great bell of Notre Dame struck midnight. Silently, and with a waking man's curiosity, he counted the strokes, nodding his head at each one, and thinking to himself that it would be five or six of the morning, and time for him to be about. But when the clock went on to tell the hour of twelve, an exclamation burst from his lips.

"*Mort Christ!*" said he to himself, "I have not slept an hour. I might know that by the music below. Saint Paul! what throats they have!"

No man cares to be deceived with the tricks of sleep; nor was Coq le Roi, — otherwise the Little Red Man, otherwise Jacques Cabot, the notorious scourge of the highways about Paris, and one of the most successful robbers that ever set spurs to a horse, — an exception to the rule. He concluded that he had a personal grievance against the night for thus cheating him. He began to tell himself that he was thirsty, and would do well to draw on his boots and venture out to a cabaret for a cup of wine. Then he remembered that he was not in the habit of losing his sleep because a few cut-throats bawled beneath the window of his garret. Some strange sound, some unusual omen of the night, must have troubled his ears while he slept, he said. And for the first time for many a day he began to remember that the guards of the new Lieutenant of Police were then hunting for him out in the woods beyond Fontenay.

"*Sang bleu!*" he cried, springing suddenly from his bed, and going to the window of his garret that he might look down thence to the narrow street below, "am I a woman that I should start at shadows on the wall? What a thing to tell — at the house of the Red Cock too!"

He put his head out of the window, and the moving panorama of the slum below reassured him. There, in the heart of the thieves' quarter of the Paris of 1761, he might well think himself safe even from the early energies of Monsieur de Sartines who had just come to be Lieutenant of Police. Though the day had begun with driving sleet and bitter wind, few of the beggars in that Rue St. Sauveur thought of sleep, or indeed of anything but their pleasures. Regularly, when night fell, these rogues whom Coq le Roi now looked down upon with satisfaction, hastened to quit the church doors and the gates of the hôtels, and hurried to the labyrinth of filthy lanes and tottering houses which had marked their kingdom behind Rue Mauconseil almost since Paris had risen about the islands of the marshes. A motley group they were; blind men counting their sous; lepers washing off their sham sores; lame men carrying their crutches; orphans cursing their fathers and mothers, who cursed them back again; venders of oranges with their cry, "Portugal, Portugal;" rogues whom the gibbet long had claimed in vain. Weary with the labours of the unbefriending day, eager for the shelter of the cabaret, ripe for quarrel, or drink, or play, they now rioted in the security of the alleys behind the markets, and so hid from the night of the greater Paris, the cankering sore, which was her reproach by day.

Coq le Roi permitted the bitter wind to blow upon his face for some minutes, then he drew back his head, for he remembered his intention to drink a cup of wine at the nearest cabaret, and he found the idea a very good one.

"Bah!" said he to himself, as he tugged at his long boots and looked to his pistols, which lay, ready for priming, upon the table by his ragged bed, "what have I to do with woman's tattle here?

Guards in the Rue St. Sauveur! what a day that would be! I should like to see it."

The notion amused him, and he chuckled to himself pleasantly; but of a sudden the laugh died down upon his lips, and he sat upon the bed like one petrified. He had become aware, in that instant, of the presence of another in the room, — a gaunt figure dressed from head to foot in black, and masked so closely that even his eyes were not visible. Noiselessly, with no drawing of bolt or creak of foot, the apparition had come to his bedside. The robber feared nothing human — but now he trembled so that the whole bed shook, and the sweat fell in icy cold drops from his brow down upon his naked chest.

"God have pity, who are you?" he asked, not daring so much as to raise his hand to the pistol beside him.

The stranger laughed merrily, and crossing before the robber, he sat himself down upon a rough oak bench which was the only seat, other than the bed, in the miserable attic. Coq le Roi could see by the little light which fell through the lattice that the visitor wore very good clothes, and that the hilt of his sword was a-glitter with diamonds.

"*Bon soir*, Monsieur Jacques Cabot," said the man, leaning back against the wall, and crossing his legs for comfort, — "*Bon soir;* or perhaps I should say rightly, *Bon jour.* The clock has just gone twelve, I think."

Coq laughed nervously. He was ashamed now that he should have so carried himself.

"I thought you were the devil," said he.

The man neglected to see that he was unanswered.

"You are an early riser, Monsieur Cabot," he continued playfully, "to be out of your bed at midnight. What a monk you would make!"

The robber shrugged his shoulders, and since he feared his visitor no longer, he stretched out a hand and took up one of his pistols. In the same moment the man in the mask gave a sharp lunge with his foot, and so cleverly was it done that the pistol went flying up to the roof and there exploded with a crash like that of cannon.

"Imbecile," said he, "would you fire upon one who comes to save your neck?"

Coq le Roi sank back upon the bed with a sigh. After all, he said to himself, there was something uncanny about the coming of this mask.

"Well," he asked doggedly, "and what next?"

The man rose and opened the window.

"This is no time for words," said he; "let your ears tell you the tale."

He held up his hand warningly, bidding the

other to listen; and while the two stood there at the little casement a strange sound arose above the hum of the city life. It was a sound neither of beggars brawling nor of rogues at their play. When it had continued a little while, there was added to it the loud rattle of musketry, the clash of swords, and the tramp of many feet; while clear above all, and resounding like the note of a trumpet, was the cry, "The guards, the guards!"

"You hear," exclaimed the unknown, drawing back from the window, "our friends, the cutthroats, are welcoming the guards of the new Lieutenant of Police. Shall I tell you, Monsieur Cabot, how many years it is since a dragoon dared to pass the Virgin's statue? You have no love for history, you say. Saint Denis, I do not wonder at it, since it is for you that Monsieur de Sartines has brought about this pretty play and come into this den of beasts."

Coq le Roi, quickened by the danger, began to prime his second pistol. His natural courage had returned to him now. Little man that he was, little and with a face like a young girl's, he had made danger so good a bedfellow that surprise was rather pleasant than alarming to him.

"Bah!" cried he, "that Sartines should be such a fool as to look for me at the house of the Red Cock. Oh, we shall have a merry night, comrade

LIBERTY OF THE RED MAN

— yet who you are and why you are here, the devil take me if I can say."

He buttoned his cloak around his shoulders with itching fingers, convinced, though he did not say so, that this man who had come to him so mysteriously had come as a friend. Meanwhile, the whole quarter without was thundering with the clamour of the mob — hell itself seemed to have been loosed in that labyrinth of crime and squalor.

Coq le Roi was sure that his liberty was a matter of moments.

"Look you, my friend," he continued to the unknown, who had watched him with some amusement and perhaps a little malice, "I am now going upstairs to get some fresh air upon the roof. But I shall not forget that you, whoever you may be, warned me of to-night's affair. I wish you good-night, monsieur. When we meet again it may be your turn to thank me and to tell me how you got into this house. I hope it will be so."

The stranger laughed aloud, insolently indifferent to the haste of the other.

"You are going on the roof, Monsieur Cabot?" he exclaimed mockingly; "surely that is very thoughtless of you."

"And why, monsieur?"

"You shall be the judge of that when I tell you that five of Sartine's men are there before you."

Coq le Roi swore a full-mouthed oath. He even thought for a moment that this man had betrayed him; but he was too wise to act upon his suspicions.

"I shall see for myself," said he, and with that he quitted the room, only to return a moment later with a face white with fear.

"Monsieur," said he, trying to force a jest, "you reckon well. There are exactly five of Sartines' men above us. How many there may be in the street below, I will not venture to hazard. Nor will I dispute with you any longer. If you come here to aid me, this is the time to do your work; but if you are upon any other errand — then God help you, for I will certainly blow out your brains."

The stranger laughed again.

"I do not keep my brains in the ceiling of your garret," said he. "Upon my word you are a very impertinent fellow, Monsieur Cabot. I am half of the mind to leave you to Sartines, who has sworn to dig up the stones of Paris rather than lose the pleasure of your company."

"He has sworn that?" muttered Coq le Roi, beginning to tremble again.

"As I say. Did you not stop the coach of Madame Geoffrin but a week ago and wound two of her lacqueys? Very well, Madame Geoffrin complained to the king and the king to Monsieur de Sartines. And now, you see, the dragoons are coming to beat in the door of your house. Oh, the lieutenant knows well that he could only take you with dragoons. What a man he is — to trap you here like a bear in a cage! For you are trapped, Monsieur Cabot. Yon street is as full of police as an orange of pips. And hark, there are the troopers themselves."

The clamour without, a clamour in which were commingled the hoarse cries of men, the shrieks of women, the ringing of hoofs upon the flags, the clash of steel, the loud note of command now rose up from the street below them. Coq le Roi listened to the hubbub and his knees quaked under him; but the unknown, who had timed his play to the ultimate moment, seemed at last to turn from his humour and to take pity on the trembling robber.

"Come," said he, " follow me and ask nothing. You have a lantern there — bring it."

The hunted man was now as clay in the hands of this maker of mysteries. He lighted his lantern mechanically; mechanically he followed the stranger down the dark and narrow stairs of the house of the Red Cock. He could hear those without beating already upon his door; but he trembled no longer. The man who went before him seemed to fill him with a new courage, as a measure is filled with wine. He did not ask, "Whence does he come, whither does he go?" He said only, "He will save me." And when at length he found himself out in the narrow, high-walled courtyard which was called by courtesy his garden, he was like a child obeying a father, and trusting him unquestioningly.

"Monsieur," he exclaimed with humble civility, "there is no door to the street here."

"You lie," said the stranger, curtly; "give me your lantern."

Coq le Roi watched him with amazement now. When he had taken the lantern in his hand, he walked straight to the mouth of the old well, which was the one conspicuous thing in that filthy and deserted court. Then he unwound a long coil of thin rope, and attaching the lantern to this, he lowered it into the orifice. Coq le Roi, looking over his shoulder timidly, watched him as one watches a conjuror at his tricks.

"Monsieur," cried he, "you cannot hide me in the well."

The unknown laughed scornfully.

"St. Denis," exclaimed he, "that a man should live five years in a house and yet know nothing of its resources! Do you follow the path of that light, my friend? Well, tell me what you see."

"The light shows me walls green with slime

and fungus," said the robber. "I see great gaps where bricks have been; there are lizards of strange shapes, and rats feeding — and now I see the water. Holy Virgin! — you would not send me down there, monsieur?"

"Look again," cried the other, unmoved at the plea, "upon the right-hand side of the well at a little distance above the water's edge, — what see you now?"

Coq le Roi stretched out his neck and searched the fœtid depths with eager eyes. The twinkle of the light below was like a star seen through a black tube. The rats fled at its light; stones fell with resounding splashes while they ran; cold air oozed up and seemed to freeze the robber's face.

"*Mon Dieu!*" said he, "you have discovered something, monsieur; there is a little tunnel running into the well, and the water does not cover its mouth."

"You have said well," answered the unknown; "through that tunnel we shall pass to our friends. After you, Monsieur Cabot. The rope which holds the bucket will bear the weight of three men. Trust your life to it rather than to your friends without. I wait for you."

Coq le Roi shuddered.

"Holy Virgin!" said he, "I dare not go down there."

"You dare not — do you hear those blows? They are from the sabres of the guards who beat in your door. Shall I leave you to receive your guests? I give you one minute."

He folded his arms and waited. Coq le Roi, now wringing his hands, or running to and fro in his distress, or peering with a horrid fear into the well below, was like a woman distracted.

"God have pity," cried he; "I cannot — I cannot."

"The half of a minute is gone," answered the unknown in a voice hard as iron.

"Do you wish to kill me, Monsieur?" moaned the robber.

"You have ten seconds yet," cried the unknown.

"You torture me," wailed the robber.

"The guards are just beating in your door," replied the unknown.

It was as he said. The great iron-bound gate was giving way to the crashing blows which fell upon it. Coq le Roi listened for one long instant — and then, reeling, staggering toward the well, he clutched the rope and began to descend.

"When you come to the tunnel, kick against the wall, and that will swing you in," cried the masked man, bending over to watch him; "leave the lantern until I follow."

"You will find my Body," howled the Robber.

"You will find my body," howled the robber from the darkness.

Lowering himself hand under hand, Coq le Roi descended to the well. The unknown waited until he had reached the light, and had entered the dark hole above the water. Then he, too, clutched the rope — but he could not keep back the laugh from his lips.

"*Ventrebleu!* Sartines," said he to himself, "a merry night to you, and a merrier day to-morrow. To be fooled by a woman at your time of life! Oh, you amuse us finely."

"Are you coming, monsieur," roared Coq le Roi below, "Oh, for pity's sake, be quick!"

The unknown hesitated no longer, but swung himself cleverly upon the rope and so disappeared into the darkness of the well.

Five minutes later a terrible cry, like a cry of victory, arose suddenly from the ranks of the sweltering mob gathered in the narrow alley before the house of the Red Cock. From lane to lane, and street to street, it spread until it was echoed in long-drawn hooting even across the frilling waters of the Seine.

"Coq le Roi has escaped! *Holà! Holà! Holà!* Coq le Roi is free. Long life to the little red man. *Viva!* Down with the guard. *À bas,* Sartines! *Holà! Holà!*"

Loud, terrible, long sustained was the cry.

QUEEN OF THE JESTERS

Exhilarated at these unexpected tidings, spurred to new courage by the joyous news, the mob fell upon the sulking troopers with any weapon that came to its hand; and in the stifling courts and alleys there was soon to be heard the shrieks of dying men, the booming of muskets, the shriller wailing of the women. Yet it was not until dawn broke that the beggars began to number their dead, and to forget that Coq le Roi was free.

Monsieur de Sartines had supped well, as he always did at the Hôtel Beutreillis. Though he declared that the gloomy old house in the Rue St. Paul was more forbidding than the Bastille where its exterior was concerned, there was no one readier to admit that Mademoiselle Corinne de Montesson, its mistress, was the cleverest woman in Paris and the most fascinating. Besides, was she not the particular patron of all the rogues and vagabonds in the thieves' quarter, and could she not, if she would, be of more service to the court in general and to himself, Monsieur de Sartines in particular, than a squadron of dragoons? It was a big " if," since mademoiselle's charity and large-heartedness were traditions in the city; but the lieutenant still hoped — and supped.

On this particular evening, the excellent man had much need of consolation, and of the rich red wine which added the lustre of the ruby to the sparkling Venetian glass in which Corinne's guests were always served. For it was the evening of the day when Coq le Roi had slipped through his fingers in so miraculous a manner; and in escaping had set the whole city laughing at her Lieutenant of Police. Nor had the good Sartines secured at that time the reputation which in after years brought him fame beyond the fame of any who had occupied the office which he glorified. He had yet to prove himself; and in proving himself he had begun with this disastrous and long-remembered fiasco.

Depressed by the reflection, gloomy, and not a little irritable, he had gone to Mademoiselle de Montesson's house, scarce daring to hope that she would aid him; convinced, none the less, that she would amuse him. He had found her, to his satisfaction, alone save for the presence of her wonder-loving old physician, Antonio, and of her young kinsman, Bénôit, who was said to be the finest swordsman in Paris. The supper had been unsurpassable, as it was always at the Hôtel Beautreillis; and when it was done, mademoiselle carried her guest to the great music-room, and there caused her servants to bring the delicious coffee of the East. And this being served, Hátrin, her harpist, began to touch the strings of his instrument caressingly; while mademoiselle herself, sharing a rest-giving lounge with the gloomy lieutenant, endeavoured to play wittily upon his melancholy.

"I read your thoughts, my dear friend," said she.

"They would make a dull book, mademoiselle," replied the other.

"Oh, not at all; such a book has yet to be finished. Gloom is the seasoning which gives joy its savour, Monsieur de Sartines — just as failure is the salt which provokes the appetite for success."

"Of what are you thinking, my dear lady?"

"I — of what should I think but the happiness of my friends? And you are not happy, monsieur. Indeed, you are the picture of misery."

"And you are of merriment, mademoiselle — and of beauty."

The lieutenant bowed pompously when he uttered the compliment. Mademoiselle herself laughed a rippling girlish laugh — she had lived but twenty-three years, and the fountain of her youth still played abundantly.

"Ho, ho," she cried, "a compliment from Monsieur de Sartines. I shall look for the question next. You will spare me the torture of the boot, monsieur."

"It would have to be a very pretty boot, dear lady."

"Another compliment. Oh, surely, Monsieur de Sartines is about to put the question."

LIBERTY OF THE RED MAN

"How! You think that I have something to ask — of you?"

"And why not? There would be stranger questions."

"You must prove that before I admit it."

"Certainly, I will prove it in a word. You came here to-night to speak about Coq le Roi."

Monsieur de Sartines, when he heard this, sat straight up like a man who has been hit in the back with the flat of a sword.

"*Pardieu!*" cried he, "what do you know about Coq le Roi?"

She laughed at him girlishly and very sweetly.

"I know much more than the Lieutenant of Police," she said.

"You are pleased to jest, mademoiselle."

"I — to jest — what an accusation!"

"Then convince me that you do not."

"With the greatest pleasure possible — for instance, you would like to learn —"

The lieutenant laughed savagely.

"I would like to learn where the man is at this moment," exclaimed he.

"Is that all — surely, nothing could be more simple. I will summon Antonio."

"Oh! it is Antonio who is the friend of assassins, then?"

"Certainly, he is a brother to them all. Does that shock you, dear Monsieur de Sartines? If so, we will not trouble him."

"By no means," cried the lieutenant, who was boiling over with curiosity; "at least he will amuse me."

"I promise that," replied Corinne.

Sartines had expected that she would rise from her seat to summon the physician as she had promised; but she did not so much as move a finger; and when some minutes had passed the lieutenant became impatient.

"Well," he said, "are you not going to exhibit this godfather of assassins?"

"Surely, since he is here now."

It was as she said. The old doctor, Antonio, had entered the room during their talk; and the lieutenant felt a cold chill run down his spine, when suddenly he became aware that a strange figure stood at his side. Whence the apparition had come; from the shelter of what trap, or panel, or hiding-place, Sartines could not tell. He knew only that the old man was before him, clad in his Geneva gown, wearing a full-bottomed wig, the curls of which almost touched his elbows.

"*Ciel!*" cried he, "you have a light foot, doctor."

Antonio bowed with the grace of a prince-bishop.

"At your service, lieutenant," said he. "If all report be true, you will need many light feet for your work in Paris."

Sartines bit his lip. The physician's words seemed a reflection upon his mishap with Coq le Roi.

"Come," said he, "let us talk of other things. Mademoiselle has promised that you will amuse me —"

"I am here to obey my mistress," said the old man, — what is your pleasure, lieutenant?"

"Oh, my pleasure is not in question, but mademoiselle has said —"

"I have said that you will tell him what the highwayman named Coq le Roi, is doing to-night," cried Corinne, interrupting suddenly; "there is nothing more simple than that, eh, Antonio?"

"It is a child's task, mademoiselle."

Sartines, who had begun by treating the whole thing as an elaborate jest, listened to this talk incredulously. While he told himself that Antonio's claim was absurd, preposterous, ridiculous, nevertheless the idea that he should put the physician to the trial was strong and fascinating. He felt like one in the presence of a conjuror. He would watch the trick closely — perhaps learn something from it. Besides, if he should get any information about Coq le Roi — but that, he said, was impossible.

QUEEN OF THE JESTERS

Antonio, meanwhile, had crossed the great room and had seated himself before a little table upon which was an astrolabe in brass, a lamp with a green shade, and a large sheet of drawing-paper, all scrawled over with hieroglyphics and strange lettering like the lettering of an Eastern manuscript. When he had turned back the long sleeves of his gown, and had taken a pair of compasses in his hand, the doctor bade the others come near.

"Monsieur," said he to Sartines, "you desire to know in what occupation the man Jacques Cabot, sometimes called Coq le Roi, has been employed during the last twelve hours. If you will be good enough to sit by my side, and to say nothing until the clock shall strike again, I will tell you."

The lieutenant, assuring himself that he was a fool to take part in such mummery, sat as the physician directed. Corinne took her stand beside him; Antonio, resting his head upon his hands, cried suddenly for less light; and at the words, lacqueys entered the room noiselessly and extinguished the candles. Only the shaded green lamp remained; and from its aureole of light the figure of the old doctor stood out — motionless, stern — the figure of some weird magician risen up from the ages of the past.

Five minutes passed, and nothing was to be heard in the great room but the ticking of the clock. Sartines found himself spellbound; Corinne herself stood like a statue, scarce seeming to breathe. When, at last, Antonio broke the spell, he did so by beginning to speak in a low voice, accompanying the words with the tracing of strange lines upon the paper before him.

"Monsieur," said he, addressing Sartines, but keeping his eyes upon the paper, "at twelve o'clock to-day Coq le Roi was at Soisy robbing the coach of his lordship, the Duke of Sabran."

"*Dieu!*" cried Sartines, rising from his chair, "you say —"

Antonio, without so much as turning his head, continued to draw upon the paper. Corinne touched the lieutenant gently upon the arm, and made a sign to him that he should say nothing.

"At three o'clock," continued the physician, whose voice was now strong and clear as the note of a bell, "I find that Coq le Roi was at Gros Bois after stopping the coach of the Grand Master of Artillery, the Comte d'Eu, and robbing him of three hundred louis d'or."

"*Ventre bleu!*" cried Sartines, while he threw himself back in his chair and laughed heartily, "what a play! Oh, you amuse me very well, my dear doctor."

Antonio ignored the interruption. His head was now so near to the paper that his eyes almost touched it. His voice was the voice of a man who speaks his thoughts aloud, unconscious that any listen.

"It is six o'clock," he said, after a long pause, "and the rain falls heavily upon the road to Fontenay. I see a great hill, and at its foot the woods stretch out to meet the waters. One horseman keeps watch in the dark place of the valley. He is waiting for the coming of his highness, the Duke de Nevers —"

"Thousand devils," cried Sartines, unable to control himself, "you lie, monsieur —"

Antonio turned his head swiftly; Corinne pressed the lieutenant's arm warningly.

"Your pardon," cried Sartines, nettled at his outburst, and now pale with excitement, "but has not this jest gone far enough?"

"It is as monsieur pleases," cried the old physician, pushing his paper away from him; "he has asked me what the highwayman known as Coq le Roi has done to-day and I have told him, reading from the signs which have been given to me."

"Certainly," replied the lieutenant, "you have amused me very well; but is it not possible, monsieur, that you have not read your signs aright?"

"Oh, indeed, if you think that," cried Corinne, interrupting quickly, "why not ask Coq le Roi himself?"

"Ask Coq le Roi?"

"As I say. Had you allowed Antonio to finish his work, he would have told you that, after stopping the coach of his highness, the Duke de Nevers, Coq le Roi turned his horse towards Paris; and that, even while we were speaking of him, he entered this house, and is now my guest in the Tower of St. Paul — which, I need not tell you, lieutenant, is still part of the Hôtel Beautreillis."

Sartines heard her out, and when she had finished, his face was almost as green as the shade of the physician's lamp. The sweat poured from his brow like rain; he gnashed his teeth; he laughed with the hysterical laugh of a woman.

"Am I a child, mademoiselle," he blurted out at last, "that you should tell me such tales?"

Corinne, holding herself with great dignity, struck a gong at her side; this was her answer to him.

A lacquey answered the summons while the note was still reverberating in the hall.

"Edouard," she said to the servant, "Monsieur Jacques Cabot, is he in his apartment?"

"He arrived an hour ago, mademoiselle."

"And now?"

"He is sleeping, mademoiselle."

Corinne clapped her pretty hands.

"Could anything be better?" she said. "We will have a peep at him and apologise afterwards. Come, Monsieur de Sartines, you shall doubt no more."

She led the way from the room while the lieutenant was still gaping with his astonishment, and he, not knowing whether he stood upon his head or his heels, followed her into the courtyard of the old house, and thence across a pretty garden, darkened by great chestnut-trees and a labyrinth of bushes. The Hôtel Beautreillis, as Corinne's home was called, formed a part of the once royal palace of St. Paul; and many strange old towers and turrets and pavilions then stood in its beautiful gardens. It was to one of these pavilions that the girl now conducted Sartines; and the excellent lieutenant was not a little surprised to find two sturdy Swiss guards standing sentry at its iron-bound door.

"*Parbleu!*" cried he, "you watch your guests well, my dear lady."

"Nay," she said, "it is the king's wish."

"How? The king knows that the man is here?"

"Certainly — or rather, he knows that I await him."

Sartines asked himself for the fifth time what wine he had drunk and from what malady he suffered. Then he stumbled up the narrow stairs; and, while Corinne held aloft the lantern which a servant had given to her, he entered a small and exquisitely furnished room — and there he saw Coq le Roi.

The highwayman was no typical robber. Short to the point of absurdity, with hair as red as the sands of the sea, and clothes which spoke of long hours in the saddle, you might have taken him for a hunchback of Notre Dame or a tailor of the Rue St. Severin. All the city called him the "Little Red Man," and the title fitted him like a glove. When Sartines then saw him he was sleeping, still dressed, upon a couch; and the light from Mademoiselle's lantern, playing upon his strange little face, lit up features which might have been those of a girl. Beyond this, the man was splashed to his shoulders with mud; and two great pistols he always carried were displayed threateningly upon the table beside the relics of the admirable supper he had just partaken of.

"*Dame!*" cried Sartines, feasting his eyes upon the motionless figure of the robber, "that is Coq le Roi right enough. I could pick him from a hundred."

"Certainly you could," whispered Corinne, drawing back from the room.

"Very well," cried the lieutenant, "I am content to ask no questions, mademoiselle, but in ten minutes my officers will call for their prisoner."

"One moment, lieutenant. Be pleased first to read the king's pleasure."

At this word she held her lantern quite close to the lieutenant's eyes, and showed him a little sheet of parchment which she had brought with her from the music-room. At the foot of this there was the royal seal and the signature of King Louis. Sartines took the document with trembling hands and read these words:—

"Jacques Cabot, sometimes called Coq le Roi, is to be the prisoner of Mademoiselle de Montesson until he shall steal the diamond ring from the finger of Monsieur de Sartines."

A smile, a terrible smile, played in the eyes of the now thoroughly enraged lieutenant.

"Mademoiselle," said he, bowing low, "I congratulate you upon the farce you are playing; at the same time his majesty's wish is a command to me. I shall make it my business to see him to-morrow and to alter this."

"Very well, my dear Monsieur Sartines — but remember, it is half past ten o'clock."

"Half past ten o'clock — why should I remember that?"

"You will learn presently."

He turned upon his heel with another stately

bow, and the voices of the lacqueys were heard immediately crying for his coach. Two minutes later his horses were galloping furiously toward the Hôtel de Ville; but Corinne de Montesson was still laughing in her garden.

"Oh," she said, "if only he will go to the king!"

Monsieur de Sartines did not go to the king — that night at any rate. His first act was to call the Captain of the Guard, and to give him precise instructions for the good of Coq le Roi.

"Take a file of men," said he to the captain, "and surround the pavilion of St. Paul in the garden of the Hôtel Beautreillis. Coq le Roi, the highwayman, is there. Shoot him if he attempts to leave the place. Otherwise, keep the guard posted until you hear from me."

The captain saluted and withdrew. When he had gone, Sartines called for a cup of white wine and drank it at a draught. Then he took snuff in huge quantities, seeking vainly to compose his thoughts.

"*Dame!*" said he to himself, "what a tale to tell! That she should be the friend of assassins — And the king supports her. Either I am mad or I have dreamed the things of this night. Jacques Cabot her guest! Holy Virgin — she will burn the Bastille next!"

Long he paced his apartment, his brain burning

with his changing thoughts. Twelve o'clock rang out from Notre Dame, one o'clock was told by all the churches of Paris, and still his coach waited to carry him to his own house in the Faubourg St. Germain. At a quarter past one, when sleep had begun to battle with his perplexity, a new clatter of hoofs disturbed the silent courts of the Hôtel de Ville, and awoke him from his stupor. He had scarce started up from his chair to learn the moment of the interruption when a horseman, dripping wet and splashed from head to foot with mud, burst into his room and stood at the salute before him.

"Well," cried Sartines.

"I have the honour to inform your excellency," cried the man, "that Monsieur l'Abbé Lamotte was stopped upon the road to Choisy at half past ten to-night and robbed of a hundred crowns by the man called Coq le Roi."

"What," roared Sartines, "at half past ten! You lie, rogue — I was with Coq le Roi myself at that hour."

"It is as I say, sir — I was one of the company, and I could pick the man from a thousand."

"God deliver me from all devils!" ejaculated the lieutenant; "it was the hour she told me to remember."

Monsieur de Sartines was, perhaps, as little in

LIBERTY OF THE RED MAN

love with hag's tales and superstitions as any man in Paris; but the events of that night, the strange mysteries of it, the surprises he had known, confused his brain and distracted him until he had no longer command of his reason. While the messenger was speaking to him, he found himself looking instinctively for the diamond ring upon the third finger of his left hand. It still glistened there, and he chuckled grimly when he saw it.

"Bah!" said he, "it is the king's jest. He has posted his own guards in the Rue St. Paul, and to-morrow he will deliver up Cabot to my charge. His words prove that. 'Until he shall steal the diamond ring from the finger of Monsieur de Sartines.' *Dame!* if the liberty of Coq le Roi depends upon that, he will remain a prisoner until the day of judgment. Steal my ring — Holy Virgin, I would like to see the man who could do it!"

The thought somewhat comforted him. He determined to go to his own house and to get what sleep he could before dawn broke. He said that this report of a new outrage must be untrue, since Coq le Roi was watched by his own guards in the Rue St. Paul. He remembered that the king was still at Versailles, and that if luck were willing, he would be able to find his Majesty there in the early hours of daylight. As for the stupendous mystery now hovering about the Hôtel Beautreillis and Corinne de Montesson, his tired brain could not grapple with that. He swore when he thought of it. He recalled the days when the people had declared the girl to be a witch. He fell to sleep in his own bed at last only to dream that Coq le Roi had stolen his ring and that the king himself was wearing it.

The sun had been up an hour, when the lieutenant awoke from his troubled sleep. He found his valet standing at his bedside, profuse in apology for the intrusion.

"I am sorry to disturb your excellency," he said, "but there is a mounted messenger below who has news which will not wait."

"Send him up," cried the lieutenant, springing from his bed, and beginning to dress hurriedly. "Does he come from the provost?"

"I know nothing," said the man, "save that he craves audience."

A moment later, the messenger, one of the new guard, was saluting his chief.

"I am to tell you, sir," said he, "that Coq le Roi, the highwayman, was seen this morning in the woods beyond Yères."

"Oh," cried the lieutenant, bristling with anger, "you come to tell me that — then tell it to the devil."

The man crossed himself devoutly.

"God save us all!" said he; "here is your excellency's own guard in the Rue St. Paul declaring that the fellow has slept all night and has never so much as turned in his sleep."

The lieutenant waited to hear no more. Refusing even the coffee which his servants offered to him, he called for his coach and set out at a gallop for Versailles. No fool under any circumstances, this mystery seemed to be making a fool of him. He told himself while he drove that all Paris would be laughing at him before night fell. He could have wagered his life that he had seen Coq le Roi fast asleep in the turreted pavilion of Corinne's house. He declared either that he had dreamed the thing, or that these new stories were false. The king had made the robber a prisoner in this way for some secret purpose. That purpose he must find out. Perhaps, after all, it was only his Majesty's love for a pair of pretty blue eyes.

He arrived at Versailles at eight o'clock, but learnt to his chagrin that the king had set out to the hunt, and was not to return to the palace until the afternoon. This was an irritating foil to his plans; but he spent the day in seeking audiences of his friends, and endeavouring vainly to glean some hints from which he could forge a key to his perplexity. Disappointed in this, he conceived the notion of walking a little way into the park; and so of catching his Majesty before he was surrounded by the host of idlers and pleasure-seekers who lay waiting to whisper a word into the royal ear.

It was nearly five o'clock in the evening when he set out on this quest; and an unusual stillness reigned in the magnificent gardens of the château. Here and there, daintily coloured lanterns gave dancing light beneath the trees; a few richly dressed fops were making love to pretty women; but the great world of pleasure was resting until the zenith of the night should awake it to new occupations. Sartines, indeed, found himself almost alone, when absorbed in his unending speculations he crossed the gardens where the fountains foamed redly in the glowing rays of the setting sun, and passed down the Avenue de Trianon into the groves of the more open park. This was quite deserted at such an hour. Valets, stablemen, gardeners — all were taking what rest they could, knowing well that the night would have need of them. The silence and the twilight suited the lieutenant's mood well. He began to pace a deserted avenue of yew elms with the slow steps of a man bearing a burden of worry and of doubt. He looked often across the park for the advance guards of the royal party. He believed himself to be alone, and even spoke his thoughts aloud.

" Bah!" said he, remembering still the letter

which Corinne had read to him, " when any highwayman shall steal my ring, then will I hang myself from the king's bed-post. What an idea to suggest! It really amuses me — it really — ha, ha! — "

To his surprise, a mocking laugh answered his spoken thoughts. He turned round swiftly, abashed at his words, to find that the intruder was no other than an exceedingly pretty girl, apparently not yet twenty years of age, who was then sitting upon a mouldy stone bench under the shadow of the elms. She was dressed in an exquisite riding habit of green velvet, and the merriment of her laugh, together with the brightness of her eyes and the exceeding suppleness of her figure, completed a picture which arrested even the wandering attention of the Lieutenant of Police.

"A thousand pardons, mademoiselle," cried he, bowing very low, "have I the honour — ? "

"Oh," said the young girl, laughing again, "the honour is mine, monsieur — to be forgotten by the chief of his Majesty's police."

"I see so many faces," pleaded Sartines, gallantly, "but that I should forget your face, mademoiselle — oh, that were impossible."

"I think not, monsieur — since you do not remember that you met me at the château of the Comte d'Eu."

The name of the Comte d'Eu sent a shiver down the lieutenant's back. It recalled the old physician and his mystic prophecies.

"*Pardieu!*" cried he, "I remember, of course. You are a kinswoman of the count's, I doubt not — and that being so, you know something of the misfortune which overtook him yesterday."

"Indeed, I do," said the girl, "since I was with him in his coach when he was stopped by the highwayman they call Coq le Roi."

Sartines gasped. Such a striking confirmation of the old physician's words he had never looked to hear.

"Mademoiselle," cried he, very anxiously, "will you permit me to sit a moment while you tell me more of this affair?"

She made way for him readily upon the bench.

"Oh," she said, "I will tell you anything you please — and I know a good deal more about Coq le Roi than you do, Monsieur de Sartines."

The lieutenant looked at the girlish figure beside him and laughed a little contemptuously.

"You must convince me of that," said he.

"Certainly I will — though I ought not to do so. It is dangerous to play with other people's secrets, Monsieur de Sartines."

"Secrets," exclaimed the lieutenant, "why — what secrets can there be in a case like this?"

"If I were sure we were alone, I might be tempted to tell you. But look how dark it grows. Upon my word I must not stay any longer, monsieur — another time you shall learn all."

Sartines' eagerness was now beyond control.

"Indeed," said he, "I beg you will do me the favour to remain, if it is only for ten minutes. Are you not safe with me?"

"I should be — but you know it is lonely here — and hush, is there not some one coming?"

They both listened a moment, but the murmur of the fountains and the echo of distant music were the only sounds in the darkness of the grove.

"Well," resumed Sartines, "you see that we are alone — and now, I beg of you — "

The girl sighed — a sigh of regret and hesitation.

"It is very wrong of me," she said, "and Corinne will never forgive me."

"Corinne!" ejaculated the lieutenant, "do you refer to Mademoiselle de Montesson?"

"Certainly."

"And what of her?"

The girl appeared to hesitate, and it was only after a long pause that she said: "Oh, she has been very unkind to you. She made a wager with the king that she would find an actress from the Opéra Comique and pass her off on you as Coq le Roi himself. And she has won, you know!"

"What!" roared Sartines.

"It is as I say. The man you thought you saw in her house last night was not a man at all. It was Mademoiselle Guérin, from the Opéra Comique."

"Thousand devils," exclaimed the lieutenant, rising from his seat, "I never thought of that!"

"Of course you did not. You forgot that your robber has the face of a young girl. Corinne, you know, remembered that, and so she tricked you. She has always been the friend of Coq le Roi. She warned him two days ago that spies were in the Rue St. Sauveur, and lent him the disguise in which he escaped. He told her himself what coaches he was going to rob and where. Her old physician helped her with his nonsense and his gown. And now she has set all Paris laughing at you."

Sartines groaned like a wounded man.

"What, then, in heaven's name means this farce about stealing my ring?" he cried, more to himself than to the pretty creature at his side.

"My dear Monsieur de Sartines, where are your wits?" said the girl. "Don't you see that she wishes to get the king's pardon for her friend? And the king makes this ridiculous condition, meaning that the man shall not be pardoned. Oh, it is all as plain as the Trianon there."

"Of course it is, of course it is," snarled the lieutenant, whose hands were trembling with rage and shame.

"I could tell you many more things, monsieur," continued the girl, "if the sun were not in such a hurry to set — but see how dark it grows. Meanwhile, here is a letter which you may keep and read when you return to Paris to-night — it will tell you much."

She took a letter from the breast of her habit and pressed it into the hand of the lieutenant, allowing her fingers to rest for some moments in his. Sartines, tormented by a thousand reproaches, did not even notice the pressure.

"Do you know," he asked abstractedly, "in what disguise Coq le Roi left the Rue St. Sauveur?"

"Indeed I do, monsieur; it was in the disguise of a woman of fashion, — in fact, he wore a green velvet riding-habit which Corinne gave to him."

"A green velvet riding-habit," repeated Sartines, thinking of anything but the green velvet habit at his side.

"Nothing else, — a green velvet riding-habit and a little three-cornered hat. Oh, they cheated you well — but read that letter, and it will save you being fooled a third time."

"A third time!" exclaimed the lieutenant, looking round quickly, while the clasp of the girl's pretty fingers was strong upon his left hand, into which she was forcing the letter.

"As I say — a third time," she explained boisterously. " Corinne has cheated you once in making you believe that a woman is a man; I have cheated you a second time in making you believe that a man is a woman."

Her words came in a torrent; and even while they were upon her lips, she raised the gloved hand which was free, leaving the other hand still in that of the man; and very dexterously and suddenly she cast the contents of a tiny bottle she had concealed in her palm into the eyes of Monsieur de Sartines. At the same moment she grasped his fingers with a strange twist, and so sprang to her feet. But the lieutenant, whose eyes seemed on fire and who believed himself to be blind, roared like a stricken bull.

"Who, in heaven's name, are you?" he cried.

"I am Jacques Cabot, otherwise Coq le Roi, otherwise the Little Red Man — very much at your service. *Bon soir*, Monsieur de Sartines. You will see very well in ten minutes. I have your diamond ring upon my left hand."

The lieutenant uttered a terrible cry and staggered across the path, in a vain endeavour to grapple with the robber. But when the guard at last answered his cries he was quite alone, and the silence of the night reigned in the grove.

A PRISON OF SWORDS

III

A PRISON OF SWORDS

JACQUES DE SERREFORT was sleeping when the jailor opened the door of his cell; but he awoke while the keys still rattled in the lock, and sat up in his bed half blinded by the sunlight which streamed through the high window of his prison. It was a morning of early June, fresh with sweet breezes of the summer and the odour of roses in the air; but the captive, who had lived a day of the long ago in his dreams, regarded neither the hour nor the freshness of it. Every morning for fifteen years had he arisen from such dreams of the old time to forget them quickly in the terrible realities of his doom. The gentle smile upon his face, born of the visions of the night, passed at once in the first moments of the day. Sleep had carried him to the fair fields of Brittany, to the pastures of his homestead, to the ingle wherein his wife, and the daughter he had loved more than life, had been wont to greet him when the day's work was done. But the dawn destroyed illusions so welcome. He became the slave again. Nothing to him that it was the height of summer, when all Paris was alive with merry music and feasting and the notes of bells calling lovers to the altars. Day or night, the fall of the leaf or the flowering of the blossom — the hour was long since passed when he remembered these. No more did he rave against the destiny which had made him a perpetual prisoner in the Conciergerie. His mind was rusted from long disuse; he talked and acted like a little child; tears refused him their consoling friendship. He prayed that the end might be soon; he sorrowed only because death was not given to him.

The jailor entered the cell as he had entered it every morning during those terrible years. He and Serrefort had grown old together; old in association, almost in captivity. True, Baptiste, as they called the fellow, had a little house out in the cathedral close yonder, and went there at odd hours to gossip with his neighbours; but nine-tenths of his years were spent in the Conciergerie, and he knew every stone in it, nay, almost every crack in its tremendous walls. In his way, he had been a good friend to Jacques de Serrefort — a friend in the little things of kindness whose worth to a prisoner is inestimable. Every morning, as soon as the bells of Notre Dame struck six o'clock, he would enter the wretched man's cell to cry: "Courage, comrade; here is the day. Who knows what it will bring?" Jacques would declare sometimes that he had said the same thing every day for fifteen years. But it came out of the goodness of his heart, and was not to be resented. Indeed, the prisoner welcomed the sound of the homely voice; and when on this particular morning of June, in the year 1761, the customary greeting was not given, Serrefort turned quickly to his jailor with a question upon his lips.

"How now, Baptiste," cried he, "you are silent this morning!"

Baptiste shook his head, and went toward the window that Serrefort might not see his face.

"Courage, comrade," said he; "it will not be for long — your daughter will return to Paris presently, and then all will be well."

Serrefort, who had begun to dress, sat down upon his bed again. He divined that some great misfortune was about to overtake him, though of its nature he could foresee nothing.

"Come, Baptiste," said he, "you speak in riddles. What has my daughter to do with the Conceirgerie — have I not enough to bear that you should talk of her?"

"*Dame!*" replied the old jailor, "I must speak of her since she alone has kept you from the

Bombec Tower[1] these two years and more. Think you, comrade, that the bailiff gives windows and red wine to all who ask them? Saint Denis, you have the best quarters in the prison, and the best food. And why? — why, because your daughter has paid for such things. You don't know that?"

"I swear to heaven that I know nothing," exclaimed Serrefort. "You say that I have these things through my daughter, and that she pays for them?"

"How else should you have them? *Sapristi!* a child would not be so simple. She has paid for them since your old protector, the Sieur Buchot, died. And she will pay for them again — when she comes back to Paris. Oh, be sure of it. She is a good child, and rare is the week when she does not tell me what she means to do for you. Do not lose heart, old friend. Who knows? — she may be ill or gone away upon an affair of importance.

---

[1] AUTHOR'S NOTE. — The Bombec Tower, it may be well to point out, was that tower of the Conciergerie prison in Paris in which torture was generally inflicted. I have added nothing in this story to historical descriptions of the cells in this horrible place. It was not until the end of the last century that these sunless dungeons were altered radically. At that time, the swords in the walls, and the loathsome creatures which the Seine washed into the cells, were still the talk of the curious.

A PRISON OF SWORDS

If the bailiff were reasonable, he would think of these things. But he will not hear me, and the order now is that I am to carry you to the Bombec Tower this morning, and to show you no more favours until you can pay for them again."

Serrefort shuddered. He had not lived in the great prison for fifteen years without hearing many a grim story of the terrible *oubliettes* below the level of the river Seine, wherein, shut out from God's day and surrounded by horrors unnameable, the more wretched and poorer victims of the bailiff Hubert's greed went all too slowly to their doom. Captivity is apt to obliterate from a man's heart those finer affections which are fed upon freedom. Serrefort was tempted for a moment to bitter thoughts of the daughter who had left him to a fate so horrible. But anon he remembered Baptiste's words, that she must be ill or away upon an affair of importance. And then he complained no more, but fell to wondering what her life had been since he had left her, a child of fifteen, in the old home in Brittany. He could not forget altogether that he owed this enduring punishment to her, and her alone. The hardness born of prison life closed about his heart when he told himself that if he had not struck the man who had been the shadow upon her life, he would not now be a prisoner in the Conciergerie. Such thoughts, however, passed upon the instant, and his great love of her came flowing into his heart like a freshet, and he longed, with the accumulated longing of years, to take her to his heart again.

"Lord, let me see her once more," he prayed, and so praying he dressed himself and told Baptiste that he was ready.

"Old friend," said he, "I have been blind indeed, to take these gifts from the hand of one whose own need must be so great. Think you that I would have permitted Irène to work for me at a time when she has neither friends nor helpers in all the city? Heaven forbid that I should have so little love for her. Oh, I am ready to follow you, Baptiste. I care not where you carry me if only you bring me news that she is well. Have I aught else in the world to remember but my little Irène? God shield her always in the shadow of His love."

He stood up dressed now, and the sunlight fell, bright and golden, upon his clear features and snow-white hair. He had been one of Condé's legion in the old time; a type of fine manhood and dashing courage. They said that there was no finer swordsman in the regiment; no better horseman. Nor had fifteen years of captivity robbed him altogether of that magnificent figure and soldierly carriage which had been the envy of his comrades in the long ago, when Brittany was the fairest country in the world to him, and the face of his young wife the sweetest face in all France. He stood up now, the sun showing the pallor of his face and the deep black lines beneath his eyes; but his body was erect, his shoulders square, his step firm. And so, like a soldier upon parade, he quitted the cell which had harboured him so long, and followed Baptiste to the corridor without.

There was a file of men in the passage armed with harberds and spontoons; a little army to guard a prisoner, who had never in his wildest moments dreamed of escape from a citadel so formidable as the Conciergerie. Serrefort exchanged no greeting with them; but he surveyed them with some scorn when they closed about him and began to march down the corridor, and so to the head of a flight of steps which appeared to lead into the very bowels of the earth. For one short instant a window showed him the city, and beyond that the river, bright with lapping green waves and busy boats, and the houses all huddled together in the sunlight, and the streets full of hurrying throngs, glad because the new day had come. He said that the world lay there, — the world where men hoped and loved and worked; the world he would never know again. And then the window was passed, and he found himself descending the winding stairs

of the great Bombec Tower, which seemed to rise
up from the very river itself. Though his guards
held torches high above their heads, the place was
so dark that even the garish yellow light could not
penetrate the terrible blackness. Serrefort feared
almost to set foot upon the ground, lest he should
tumble into some horrid pit or go headlong into
the waters of the Seine. So heavy and damp was
the air that his lungs seemed to be filled with noxious vapours at every breath. Even the floor of
the staircase was covered with wet and slime, while
water dripped from the walls in a ceaseless " pat-
pat-pat," which spoke eloquently of the surpassing
misery of those who must live in depths so terrible.
Serrefort had heard often of the Bombec Tower.
He remembered that when as a little child his
father had brought him to Paris, they had shown
him this great stone bastille, one of the towers of
the Conciergerie springing up from the very river's
bed, and they had spoken in hushed voices of the
suffering of those doomed to such a prison. And
now he must learn of these things for himself.
Indeed, the lesson had begun already when the
sunshine was left far above him; and an intolerable longing for air and light forced him to say that
he must lose his reason if they did not carry him
up again to the day he had left. And so he came
to the foot of the staircase, and his guards having

A PRISON OF SWORDS

gone some little way down a narrow and sinuous passage, one of them held a torch aloft, while old Baptiste unlocked the door of a cell and bade the prisoner enter.

"Courage," said he, "for the love of Heaven. It is only for a little while, and your daughter will be back again. You will find a seat there — do not quit it until I come to you. It is the prison of swords you enter, God help you."

There was a quaver in the old man's voice when he spoke; but Serrefort did not hear. His eyes were staring horribly into the hole which henceforth must be his home. Bright as the flare of the torch was, its light could penetrate but a little way into that den wherein the sun's rays had not entered for centuries, nor any sound been heard but the groans and sobs of the wretched victims of the dungeon.

"Oh," cried Serrefort, pitifully drawing back, "if I might die! I cannot enter — I cannot — "

But old Baptiste cried again, —

"Courage, my son, courage; she will come back — I shall see her to-day — oh, she has not forgotten you, be sure of it."

He spoke as a father might have spoken to a son; and pushing the trembling prisoner gently forward, he closed the door upon him and hurried back to the light and the life above. Penalty enough that he should spend moments in an abode of such horrors. Serrefort, on the other hand, took two steps forward and then sank down upon the mouldy straw with which the floor of his new prison was covered. There was no braver man in Paris, none with a stouter heart nor more noble courage; but the Bombec Tower was quick to conquer him. Fear now dominated his mind, until his whole body trembled, and his very heart seemed to stand still. The darkness weighed upon him like a crushing burden. The foul cell appeared to be full of the shapes of those who had gone before him to this agony. His lungs were scorched by the stifling air; the dreadful silence, he said, was the silence of the tomb. Every moment he waited to feel the touch of some creeping thing upon his face; he crouched like a driven animal, putting out his hand to find the walls with his fingers. But his hand was cut by the blade of a knife protruding from the stone work, and as he drew it back bleeding, he remembered what Baptiste had said, that he was then in the prison of swords. Full well he knew what the words meant. Many a time had he heard of this infamous cell wherein the walls bristled with knives, and the floor of which, as tradition told, was covered with creeping things, and even with loathsome reptiles.

"Oh, my God," he prayed again, "have pity

A PRISON OF SWORDS

upon me, have pity upon me — I cannot suffer it
— I cannot!"

Maddened, as many prisoners before him, he
hurled himself ferociously upon the floor and
writhed there with burning brain, and hands and
arms cut by the sharp blades which protruded from
the walls. When the fever passed, and he lay
weak and motionless upon the straw, he began to
ask himself by what right the bailiff inflicted these
wrongs upon him. Years had gone by since he
had sinned in striking the Comte de Châteauneuf,
the lord of his province, who had robbed him of a
fame which was more precious to him than wealth,
and had sought to injure the one being for whom
he would have given his life willingly. Had they
such memories that they remembered the crime
still? He could not believe it; but as misery grew
upon him, there came back, strong and clear and
life-giving, his hate of the man who had doomed
him to such agonies. Often in his prison above
had he prayed that the day might be his when he
would meet the Comte de Châteauneuf face to face
and reckon with him for these years. His brightest dreams were those wherein he fancied that his
enemy lay dead at his feet, and that he, Jacques de
Serrefort, had the dripping sword of victory in his
hand. But these dreams were sent for his punishment, since how could he, a helpless prisoner,

revenge himself upon a man who commanded in Paris an influence no less powerful than in Brittany. He knew that it could not be; yet hoped the more, and in his hope found the will to live.

It had been very early in the morning when they carried him to the Bombec Tower and old Baptiste had brought a manchet of bread and a flask of wine to the dungeon, so that Serrefort could not hope to see his jailor again before night fell. For the matter of that, he had nothing to tell him the hour; and he lay, it seemed for days, quite still in his cell, while the rats ran over his arms, and ever and anon some living thing would touch his face and fill him with loathing inexpressible. The patter of these animals was for a long time the only sign of life down there below the river's flood; but anon he heard a gentle lapping of water, and knew that the tide was rising. It was good at the first to think of Mother Seine, which ran without like some friend of the world he had forgotten, and he took pleasure in calling to mind its aspect when last he had seen it. That was when they carried him over the Pont Neuf to prison. The river had been alive with boats then; with boats and barges, and gallant going down to Passy, and merry jesters making merry music, and all the life and brightness of the great city. To-day, he said grimly, all that world passed within a stone's

A PRISON OF SWORDS

throw of him; yet his eyes were blinded to the sights; his ears deaf to the music; he would never see that river again; the world would pass for ever by and no cry of his go out, no hand of pity be offered to him. And while this thought was in his mind, the lap of the waves grew stronger; the sound of water began to fill the whole cell. He realised quite suddenly, yet with a new, an immeasurable dread, that the river would rise above the level of his cell. When at last a cold stream of water touched his feet, he cried out anew, thinking that they meant to drown him and had brought him to the Bombec Tower with that intent.

The water rose slowly, lapping about the feet and knees and hands of the prisoner. But he had imagined a fate which was not in the minds of those who had sent him to the dungeon. Twice every day the Seine washed the floor of this cell, bringing up great rats in its flood and leaving the oozing slime and filth of its waters upon the straw which made the prisoner's bed. Just when Jacques de Serrefort was telling himself that the water would cover his mouth presently, its flow ceased, and taught him the devilish malignity of his captors. Wet and cold and shivering, the wretched man stood for long hours while the stream ebbed. Then he sank again upon his reeking bed to ask how he should support another day of torture so revolting and cruel. He could not forget that there had been prisoners who had spent long years in this very cell, who had become raving madmen and yet had lived on; sport for their jailors, but not food for death. Serrefort swore that no such fate should be his; he would find another way; he would cast himself upon the mercy of heaven and end the terror before reason robbed him of the power.

Until this time, and he judged that it must now be night, no sign had been given that those above remembered his existence. Though he listened long and called out with all his strength, he heard no answering voice, no tread in the passage without. The massive walls shut down his cries and entombed them. A fearful roof of earth seemed to weigh upon his prison and heat it with hot and choking air. Serrefort declared that he realised for the first time what anguish must be the lot of those who wake in a tomb. He would have welcomed death as a gift of mercy; but for the time being he had neither the strength nor the will to compel death. Rather he turned to think of old Baptiste's promise that he would come again; of his assurance that his daughter Irène would return to Paris to bring him the comforts of the cells above. But the hours wore on and no one came, and hope ebbed, and the fever of the cell racked his bones. He had been known ever as one who had a clear mind, quick, active, far-seeing; but the darkness of the dungeon in the Bombec already warred upon his brain. A drowsiness crept upon him, nature's medicine against his terror; he could not sleep, yet became almost insensible to the horrors of the cell; he forgot where he was; visions of his home and wife came back to him, so that when his cell door was opened presently and the flare of a torch lit up its inmost recesses, those who visited him found tears running down his cheeks and a word of love upon his lips.

Serrefort had thought when he heard the key grate in the lock that it was old Baptiste come back as he had promised; but as soon as his eyes were awake to the light, he looked up to see the bailiff Hubert, the governor of the prison, and with him a tall grey-haired man, whose fine dress and white ruffles were strange things to find in the Conciergerie. The same soldiers who had conducted the prisoner to the cell in the morning now accompanied the governor and ranged themselves on either side of the prisoner, bidding him rise and salute the bailiff. Serrefort did so mechanically, shutting his eyes that he might not behold the dreadful sights which the torches disclosed. All his old spirit was broken now; he held his head erect no more — one day in the Bombec had made him an old man.

"Sirs," said he, with a sob in his voice, " I beg of your pity carry me from this place — you see how I suffer — oh, God knows what my sufferings have been."

He stood before them sobbing like a child, fearful that they would leave him to the silence of the pit again, to the flowing waters and the maddening darkness. At any other time, his distress would have been a fine subject for merriment to the bailiff Hubert; but the man was dumb in the presence of a stranger, who did not conceal his sympathy nor hesitate to utter it.

"Monsieur," said this stranger, presently, "you are Jacques de Serrefort, I believe, sent to this place now fifteen years ago for threatening to kill Monsieur le Comte de Châteauneuf — is that so ?"

Serrefort raised his head quickly at the mention of his crime. His shoulders were squared again; he stood before them erect and fearless, as he had stood before his officers in the old days.

"Monsieur," he said, " it is quite true that I am the Jacques de Serrefort you name. Yet whether it were a crime or no which sent me to this place I leave my God to judge."

"Impudent fellow," cried the bailiff, " I will have you branded upon the face with an iron."

The stranger, who did not appear to love the bailiff, hushed him with a gesture of his hand.

"Please to hold your tongue, monsieur," cried he, with the air of one accustomed to command; "I am here to interrogate the prisoner, not to listen to your angers."

The bailiff bit his lip and scowled at Serrefort. It was with difficulty that he turned a smiling face to the stranger at last, and said as pleasantly as possible: —

"Your pardon, Monsieur le Comte. Yet have a care, I beg of you, how you deal with this fellow, for he is very dangerous."

"I will be the judge of that myself," said the man addressed as count; and then turning to Serrefort, he continued: —

"Hark you, my friend, you are not to deceive yourself with any hope that I am come here to serve you. If I carry you away from the Conciergerie to-night, it will be that I may send you back when a few hours are passed to do as the bailiff shall bid you. But first you must give me your word as a man of honour — for such I know you to be, monsieur — that you will obey me faithfully and return here when midnight is struck. Are we agreed upon that, Monsieur de Serrefort?"

Serrefort rubbed his eyes; the men, the light, the voices were unreal to him. He heard the injunction and yet could not gather the words together.

"Monsieur," cried he at last, "if you should take me out of this place, be it only for an hour, I will thank you from my heart. You know not what a place it is—oh, there is no crime which merits such a punishment as this, monsieur."

The count surveyed him with pity in his glance.

"Very well, Monsieur de Serrefort," cried he, after a moment; "we are agreed upon the bargain then. You are to have your liberty until twelve o'clock in return for some information you shall give me presently. But it is understood that you return here at midnight, and that you will not seek to escape those who accompany you. I have your word, monsieur?"

"A hundred times," replied Serrefort, to whom the thought of an hour's liberty was dear beyond price.

The count turned swiftly to the bailiff Hubert.

"Let your prisoner be taken to my carriage at once," said he; "what else is to be done you have learnt already. Is it not so?"

The bailiff stammered an answer.

"Monsieur le Comte," exclaimed he, "this is a serious matter—I have no authority from the king—and—as monsieur knows—"

"Silence!" cried the count. "Should any ask you upon what authority, answer them upon the authority of the Count de Saint Florentin and of this ring."

He held up a gold signet ring — the ring of Louis, the well-beloved king of France. That was a talisman powerful even to conquer the bailiff, who drew back with a little cry when the count spoke, and now made haste to offer his apologies.

"Sir," cried he, "had I known that you came upon the king's business, it would have been different. Hold me not to blame in that I remember my duty and the security of those intrusted—"

"Oh, monsieur," said the count, whose impatience now amounted almost to anger, "if you would remember that I wait, I would even forget all your stupidities. Lead the way, sir, and let us hear less of your pestilent tongue."

The bailiff, astounded at the rebuke and snarling with temper, commanded the guards to lead out the prisoner. Serrefort, who said still that this must be a vision of his sleep, followed the soldiers with trembling steps. Never in all his life had he known so sweet a moment as that which carried him from the foul depths of the Bombec Tower to the world above and the gentle breezes of the night. Had it not been ever in his mind that he must return to that abode of suffering when a few hours had passed, he would have said that heaven had been too good to him and that he was not worthy of such happiness. But the shadow of the dungeon lay upon him like the shadow of the living death. He thought still to hear the dreadful lapping of the water; still to feel the touch of the creeping things; still to be entombed in the very bowels of the earth, with all the weight of that mighty stone crushing him down. Nothing could free him from the loathing and the fear. He saw all things about him, the figures of the men, the torches and lanterns of the guards, the open square before the Halls of Justice, of which his prison was a part, and he said that they were phantoms of his burning brain. Nor was it different when the Count of Saint Florentin bade him enter a coach drawn up at the gates, and they drove him quickly across the Pont Neuf and to the heart of the city which he had not seen for fifteen long years. He was like a man walking in his sleep. The hum of Paris, awake to the pleasures of the night, the merry cries from the boatmen upon the river, the crowds in the streets, the flickering lamps, the great buildings — here was the world for which he had longed; but it meant nothing to him. "At midnight," he said always, — "at midnight they will carry me to the Bombec again — oh, God have mercy upon me!"

The Count of Saint Florentin, meanwhile, sat

back in his carriage and surveyed the prisoner with curious eyes. He was asking himself a remarkable question, and was busy in speculation as to the answer. And his question was this — would Jacques de Serrefort return to his cell a miserable or a contented man? "The king," said he to himself, "has wagered pretty Corinne de Montesson a thousand gold pieces and the man's liberty that she will not send him back to the Conciergerie willingly. She is to have him in her house until the clock strikes twelve. If then he confesses himself content to go back to his cell, Corinne wins the wager. Oh, it is a pretty question — yet, I make sure, she has lost it already. For who ever saw a fellow so gloomy? Saint Denis, the man is at death's door now."

The count, who was then one of the most powerful men in Paris, did not usually concern himself much about the sufferings of rogues in the Conciergerie; but something in the face of Jacques de Serrefort appealed to his pity; and beyond that, he was, like all the world, in love with Corinne de Montesson, who owned the great Hôtel Beautreillis. He began to hope that she would win her wager; though, for the life of him, he had no idea as to the way she would set about it. He, at any rate, had performed his part faithfully; and when, anon, the coach drew up before the gates of Corinne's house, he had become as much interested in the strange experiment as though his own money had been ventured upon it.

The gates of the Hôtel Beautreillis were open when the coach rolled up. Many lights shone from the windows of the great house, and it was plain that Serrefort had been expected. No sooner did the coachman rein in the horses than lacqueys came running from the house to greet the count and to help the prisoner. Serrefort, accustomed to the gloom and silence of the prison, was half blinded by the brilliancy of all he saw; deafened by the clamour and the cries of the many servants. Indeed, he stood for a spell gazing about him wildly, pitifully; and would have remained so had it not been for a lacquey who touched him upon the arm and bade him follow. And so he passed the open courtyard to a pavilion of the house just as a clock in one of the turrets chimed the hour of nine. The bell reminded him that he had three hours of liberty before him; three hours when he might live in the world and hear men's voices and forget the cell — if that were possible. But the promise only added to his gloom. "They torture me with a little liberty," he said, "to make my punishment more cruel." Nor could he imagine what strange mystery had brought him to the house. All the events of that wonderful night had put a spell upon his mind. He was like a child, obeying his master in awe and wonder.

But they had conducted him to a room in the house by this time; a cabinet with painted frieze and thick carpets, and gilded chairs and many tapers shedding a soft light. He opened his eyes when he saw the richness of the apartment, and was the more surprised when two or three servants came up and began to busy themselves with his ragged clothes.

"Monsieur," said one of the fellows, bowing with great deference, "will you be pleased to dress now? Mademoiselle waits and will sup directly."

"To dress?" cried Serrefort, wonderingly. "Where am I, then, and whose house is this that I should be carried here?"

"Oh, sir," said the man, surprised that such a question should be put, "you are in the house of Mademoiselle Corinne de Montesson, and be sure that she wishes well to you. Indeed, you are lucky to have found such a friend, monsieur."

"A friend to me," gasped Serrefort; "how then is that — you jest, sir."

The lacquey did not heed the question. Rather, he made haste to take Serrefort's coat from him and to bring him water for his hands. When this was done, he spread out a uniform upon the couch and invited his mistress's guest to put it on.

"Monsieur," said he, "my mistress thinks that you would wish to appear here to-night in the uniform of your old regiment. It is all laid out there, and I beg you to hasten, for they will sup before the clock strikes."

He indicated the articles one by one as he spoke, the coat of bright blue with the gold facings, the brass helmet, the high boots, the cunningly wrought sword. Serrefort gave a little cry of delight and hesitated no longer. His weary brain, thinking ever of the Bombec, forgot its task for a moment, and carried him back swiftly to the years when there had been no finer horseman, no more dashing trooper in all France, than Jacques de Serrefort. They said afterwards that his hands trembled, that there were tears in his eyes when he stood before the long glass and buckled the sword to his belt. It was pitiful to see his snowy white hair straggling beneath the rim of the great brass helmet, to watch the effort it cost him to square his shoulders and walk as he had walked in the years long ago. But courage came with the memories, and erect, proud, almost defiant, he turned to those who served him and declared that he was ready.

"Tell your mistress," said he, "that Jacques de Serrefort awaits her commands."

The lacquey bowed and bade him, for the second time, to follow. Had it been any other who had thrown off the veteran to ape the young man, the fellow would have laughed aloud; but there was a light in Serrefort's eyes, a boldness in his carriage, before which many a man would have quailed. The lacquey said to himself that here was a true soldier, and there was a certain pride in his voice when he threw open the doors of a vast salon and announced —

"Monsieur Jacques de Serrefort."

The great room was magnificently lighted, hundreds of tapers burning brightly in chandeliers and candelabra of Venetian work. Though the floor of it was of wood, none the less were the boards polished and waxed until they shone like glass; while the walls were hid by paintings of colossal size and all the ceiling was a blaze of mosaic. So vast was the place that Serrefort remained at the door silent in awe and wonder; but when he had stood an instant he heard a sweet young voice greeting him, and looking up, he beheld Mademoiselle Corinne herself. She was standing by a great armchair, set up like a throne at the other end of the chamber, a pretty figure superbly dressed, and surrounded by fifteen men and women, whose fine clothes and graceful manners were in keeping with the magnificence of the apartment.

"Monsieur," she said, holding out both hands, "I welcome you with all my heart to this house.

These are my friends,—the Duc de Richelieu, the Duc de Cosse-Brissac, the Comte de Vaudreuil, the Duchesse de Lauzan, the Comtesse d'Egmont—oh, make haste to know them all, for they will be your friends presently."

Serrefort was stupefied. He stood motionless, staring at the gorgeous dresses, the gold, the silver, the diamonds, of the company. Though his liberty had been offered him for a word of thanks, he could not have uttered it. Minutes, indeed, passed before emotion conquered him, and he turned away with a sob in his voice.

"Oh," cried he, "it is a dream — a dream! I shall awake presently to the darkness and the silence — God help me."

That was a cry wrought of long years of misery, and it stilled the company to a hush of deep sympathy. As for the mistress of the house, there were tears in her eyes when she advanced swiftly to the old soldier's side and took his hand in hers.

"Monsieur," she said in a low voice, "have courage, I beg of you. I am your friend; you will trust me. Were you not one of Condé's legion? Remember that and forget all else."

She raised her pretty blue eyes to his in encouragement, and spoke so tenderly that a memory of his daughter's voice came back to him. But chiefly he thought of this — that he had been one of Condé's legion, and that he wore the beloved uniform again now at the eventide of his life.

"Mademoiselle," said he, proudly, "I will remember naught but your kindness — do with me what you will."

His voice was strong now, and he faced the company unflinchingly. They, in turn, anxious only that he should forget, began to speak of trivial things; and one of them — a fine fellow who was addressed as Bénoît — came to Serrefort's side and talked to him of the old days in Germany, of the wars which had been his glory, and the triumphs he had won. And so well did the young man contrive things that when supper was ready and the company passed into a neighbouring cabinet, a pretty little room fit for the king, the prisoner had forgotten the Bombec, even the Conciergerie, and all that he had suffered there.

There were sixteen guests at the table, Serrefort being placed at the right hand of the hostess, while the old Duc de Richelieu sat opposite to him, and Bénoît upon his left hand. It was a long meal exquisitely served, and offering those rare and dainty dishes in which the cooks of the eighteenth century excelled. Two soups, a bisque of pigeon and cock's combs, a side soup of hashed capon, a quarter of veal, a partridge pie, a grilled turkey, salads, creams, rissoles beignets — the dishes were multiplied in an abundancy which was to be found nowhere at that time but in the houses of the French nobles. Serrefort discovered first that he had little relish for the delicacies; his palate had been hardened for years of coarse food and sour wine; but when he had drunk some champagne from a foaming goblet and had tasted a dish of capon, his old love for good things came back to him, and he set to work to sup as heartily as the others. As for his pretty hostess, she babbled away incessantly, telling him all the news of Paris; all the jests, the humours, the intrigues, just as though he were a freeman like the rest of them, and not a prisoner enjoying a terrible furlough. For the matter of that, he began himself to forget his condition; he ceased to ask after a while, "Why am I brought here?" He said that some trick of sleep cheated him — but the sleep was very sweet, and he would enjoy it. Nor would he let himself willingly remember that when twelve o'clock struck he must set off to his prison again. The oasis in his life was too dear; heaven had taken pity upon him, he thought, and here was the answer to his prayer.

In this spirit, he began to talk presently, adding to the anecdotes and the jests. He spoke of his old deeds with the army; of the duels he had fought and the intrigues he had known. When at last supper was done, and the guests went out to enjoy the night air in the beautiful gardens, he accompanied young Bénoît readily, and found himself almost in a merry mood. For the garden was fresh and sweet at that hour; it was good to tread the soft grass; to walk upon the white moonlit paths; to smell the strong odours of the plants. No memory of a prison came to mar that hour. He was old Jacques de Serrefort again, the pride of his regiment.

This forgetfulness endured, it might have been, for the half of an hour. Young Bénoît had brought him by this time to a little grove where an arbour stood, and old trees rich in leaf; a flowery dell hid away from the world like a pool in a forest. Here they walked awhile, earnest in merry talk; but of a sudden Serrefort stood quite still, his face paled, his hand trembled. A clock in a church near by was striking the hour. The wretched man counted the bells as one doomed to death may count them upon the morning of his execution.

"Eleven o'clock," he exclaimed at last in a hoarse voice; "you heard it strike, monsieur?"

"Certainly," answered the young man; "it is eleven o'clock, as you say, Monsieur de Serrefort. An hour yet to midnight — when we lose you, I fear. I am sure that you will remember us all the same — as we shall remember you in our affection."

Serrefort did not hear him. His face was set, his shoulders stooped again. "*Mon Dieu!*" he cried, "I cannot go back — I cannot."

Bénoît, whose heart was cut by his piteous cry, pretended not to hear it; but turning quickly to the old soldier he said: —

"Monsieur, when our friend, the Comte de Saint Florentin, brought you here to-night, he told you that my mistress counted upon you for certain information. I am sure you will serve her so far as may be possible. As the time presses, let us talk of it without delay."

Serrefort answered with an inclination of the head. His thoughts were set upon the dungeon below the river. The garden, the house, the fine people — he had forgotten them all again in his overwhelming dread of the cell. Bénoît observed his abstraction, but continued nevertheless: —

"Since you are willing, Monsieur de Serrefort, will you permit me to present to you one whose acquaintance you made in Brittany many years ago, a man who desires exceedingly to speak with you, and who is coming here to-night for that purpose?"

Serrefort bowed again.

"Sir," said he, "your mistress's wish is my wish. I knew many in the old days at Brittany, many whom I would well speak of, though, heaven knows, I shall never see them again."

"I understand that, Monsieur de Serrefort," cried Bénoît, "but the man in whom we are interested should even now be in this garden. I will go and seek him if you are content to rest here awhile."

Serrefort assented indifferently. He heard the other's words with difficulty; followed his argument at a hazard; had no mind to reason the proposition. The cool night air, the gentle rustling trees, the seclusion of the garden, brought back to his memory the years when he had known the peace of a haven like this in his own fair home at Brittany. He remembered that the sin of one man had driven him forth from that home to endure the living death of the prison. Never had his hate of the Comte de Châteauneuf, the man who had sent him to the Conciergerie, waxed so strong as it did in that instant. There was a fever in his blood at the thought of the name. "*Ciel!*" he murmured, "if I might meet him face to face before I die."

It was an angry exclamation; his hand was hot upon the hilt of his sword, while the impulse of vengeance maddened him. He uttered the name of Monsieur de Châteauneuf again and again, as he paced the path with unresting steps. When he stopped at last, a great cry frothed upon his lips, the strength of ten men filled his veins; he knew that his prayer had been answered. For Monsieur de Châteauneuf stood before him in the grove — and the two were face to face at the hour of reckoning.

The count stood before him, — a man in the prime of life, dressed as the fashion of the hour dictated, in a suit of violet silk slashed with gold, and embroidered with precious stones. A sword whose hilt sparkled with diamonds hung at his side; there were diamond buckles upon his shoes; diamond pins glittering in his snow-white ruffles. But the easy placid smile which usually characterised his handsome face lighted it no longer. He stood before Serrefort with terror shining in his eyes, with quaking knees and beating heart. Ten minutes before that supreme moment, he had entered the Hôtel Beautreillis, thinking that little Corinne had some favour to grant him. They had conducted him to the garden upon that excuse, and young Bénoît had met him and brought him to the grove. But Bénoît was at his side no longer. Mysteriously, silently, he and the other guests had withdrawn from the garden. The two men, he who had sinned and he who had suffered, stood face to face in the deserted glade, and both of them knew that this was an hour momentous beyond any they had lived.

The count was the first to speak. He had suppressed a cry at the moment when first his eyes encountered those of his victim; but now, after it was plain to him that Serrefort was mad and exultant at the meeting, he turned round, thinking his guide was still at his heels.

"Monsieur, what liberty is this?"

But no one answered him. Bénoît had vanished. It seemed to the count that the silence of death was in the place. He had the impulse to flee the garden; a stupefying fear paralysed his limbs, choked his voice; the sweat of death seemed already to gather upon his forehead. Since the day when a word of his had sent Jacques de Serrefort to the Conciergerie he had forgotten the very fact that his victim lived. Now, however, it were as though a dead man had come out of his grave to demand reckoning. As for Serrefort, the ferocity of a wild beast was upon him. Anger, joy, lust for vengeance, gave incoherency to his words. The sword with which Corinne de Montesson had armed him flashed already at the count's throat. Age, debility, long years of suffering, were powerless to mar that strength of hate and of victory. Never, in his day of youth and skill, did the trooper of Condé's legion stand up with such confidence. The ring of triumph was already in his voice; his hand was the hand of a man who knows no mercy.

"Monsieur le Comte de Châteauneuf," he cried, with terrible deliberation, "God surely has sent you here that I may kill you. Draw, monsieur, for your hour has come."

The count reeled back, crying with all his voice for help. The cry moved his antagonist to a peal of mocking laughter.

"Ha," cried he, "you would run like a lacquey, Monsieur le Comte; you who have boasted of your skill in every salon of Paris — shame on you! Must I call for a whip to beat you like a dog? — draw, I beg of you, for my patience is worn. Oh, monsieur, I have waited fifteen long years for this hour. I swear that all Paris shall not save you now."

He pressed upon the doomed man with a new ferocity, adding light blows of his sword to the stinging taunts of invitation. Châteauneuf, who saw that he had fallen into a trap, hesitated no longer, but drew his sword and sprang to the engagement. And at this, Serrefort cried out again, and then, clenching his teeth, began to fight with the cunning and the resolution of a *maître d'armes*. The night, the garden, the mystery, the

A PRISON OF SWORDS

prison — all were gone from his thoughts. He saw but one object, the pale face of the man who had sent him fifteen years ago from the happiness of his home to the grave of the Conciergerie. Hate gave him a skill which had never been his, even in the best hour of the old time. And to the strength of hate was added the terror and the confusion and the conscience of Monsieur de Châteauneuf. The count, indeed, had death at his heart from the first. He fought with trembling hand, with quaking limbs. There was ever dinning in his ears the cry — "This is the justice of God." He knew that he was to die, there in the silence of the garden; knew that the sun would never shine for him again.

Twice round the grove the men fought, Serrefort playing with the other like a beast with its prey. Though the ring of swords made strange music of the night, though the sharp cries and the fierce stamping of the two were to be heard even in the street without, the men remained alone. No witness of the deed was to be found in all the great house; the silence of desolation was upon it; little Corinne and her guests had vanished in the darkness. When, at last, the count raised his voice again to call out that he was the victim of an assassin, Serrefort answered with a yell of derision.

"Monsieur le Comte," said he, "ask help of heaven and not of men, for that shall be your last cry. Ha, you have a cunning hand, monsieur, but it cannot stand the burden of your sin. Shall I tell them that I fought with a lacquey? Never let it be said."

Goaded to madness at the taunt, the Count of Châteauneuf permitted his anger to master him. He disengaged with the skill and quickness of an old swordsman, and made to lunge in *quarte;* but his foot failed him in the heat of the feint, and before he could regain his position the sword of Serrefort was running through his heart.

"Assassin!" he gasped; but the word was choked upon his lips. For an instant, he stood quite still, with the sword cutting his flesh; then, turning sharply upon his heel, he fell headlong, and lay face downwards upon the grass.

But Serrefort, withdrawing his sword and running wildly into the lighter place of the garden, stood with the moonlight falling upon his face and tears glistening in his eyes. It seemed to him that some mighty miracle was wrought in that hour, for of a sudden men and women, and lacqueys with lanterns, came running out of the house, and that which had been a scene of desolation was now a glittering picture of life.

Nevertheless, had he no care for a pageant so

THE SWORD OF SERREFORT WAS RUNNING THROUGH HIS HEART.

strange, but standing like one in a trance, he raised his eyes to heaven and exclaimed, —

"My God, I thank Thee for this night, for surely my prison shall be a prison to me no more. Nay, Lord, I go gladly, since Thou hast given me his life."

And so saying, he fell in a swoon, and they carried him into the house.

When Jacques de Serrefort came to his senses again, he was lying upon a couch in a little pavilion of the Hôtel Beautreillis, and his daughter, Irène, had her arms about him.

"Dear father," she said, "turn not away from me. It is your daughter Irène who speaks, — she whom you loved in the long ago."

Serrefort looked at her with a loving regard. Then taking her hand as he used to do in the old days in Brittany, he exclaimed: —

"Little one, you will never leave me more?"

"Oh, never," she exclaimed, covering his hands and face with kisses. "Dear father, the king, who learnt all to-night, has pardoned you. It is Mademoiselle Corinne's work — she who owns this house and has taken pity upon us. We are to go to Brittany to-morrow, for she has the king's promise. I will never leave you more, beloved father."

But Serrefort closed his eyes again. The great clock of Notre Dame was striking twelve, and all the phantoms of the Bombec came winging into the room to torture him with a memory of that which might have been. When the hour was struck, he raised himself upon his couch and kissed his daughter.

"Little one," said he, " our God is good — let us go and thank your mistress."

AT THE HOUSE OF THE SCARLET WITCH

IV

AT THE HOUSE OF THE SCARLET WITCH

THE Abbé Morellet heard the ring of hoofs upon the dusty road behind him and instantly stopped his long-suffering white pony. He was a man of alarms, was this good abbé; and his two servants, being dutiful servants, were for the occasion men of alarms also. All three had heard strange stories of the perils of those travellers rash enough to venture after sunset upon the great Western highway to Paris; all three had begun to regret the necessity which had carried them from the peaceful presbytery near Rambouillet to the woods upon the outskirts of the great city. Yet here they were at eight o'clock of a summer's evening in the year 1762 still three leagues from Paris, with dark already threatening them, and all the tales of bogies and of robbers ringing in their ears like a passing bell in the ears of men about to be hanged.

"It is my opinion," said the abbé, addressing François, his valet, — "it is my opinion that we are followed by the three young men who delayed us at the Maison Rouge. I can see a cloud of dust upon the horizon and I count three horses."

François, the valet, and Jean, the groom, hastened in their turn to check the asses which they rode and to inspect the winding highway which they had traversed with so many misgivings. Being ready men, their tongues presently wagged together, and they declared themselves willing to submit to untold tortures if they also did not see a cloud of dust upon the horizon and count three horses.

"*Sapristi!*" cried François, the valet, "I suspected those fellows from the beginning. What says the proverb, my master? — he who makes friends in an inn has the devil for his comrade. Body of Saint John, I was for going on as your reverence is well aware."

Jean, the groom, who watched the approaching horsemen with fearful eyes, yet was unwilling to betray himself, remembered now that he had been for going on too.

"Oh," cried he, "if yon rogues are not footpads I never saw one. Did you mark how they kept their faces masked even when they sat at meat? Put me in the pillory if ever I heard of an honest man who was afraid to show his nose to his neighbour. We shall all be dead men presently, rely upon it."

"IF YON ROGUES ARE NOT FOOPADS, PUT ME IN THE PILLORY."

The abbé, who nursed a secret suspicion that the groom spoke the truth, told him nevertheless to hold his tongue. He consoled himself with the thought that his personal property was not worth a louis to any rogue; he knew that he had but ten crowns in his pouch; and those he would surrender readily. Indeed, he began to frame a little speech in which he determined both to rebuke the robbers and to conciliate them. And this was still troubling his mind when the three men rode up at a gallop, and began to parley with him. They were a strange trio — all dressed elegantly, all mounted upon horses which might well have come from the king's stable. The abbé, stealing glances at them when he lifted his eyes a moment from his breviary, did not fail to observe the shining embroidery upon their vests nor the rich ruffles falling delicately upon their wrists, nor the diamonds glistening upon their fingers. These things had been hidden from him in the dark room of the tavern at Sèvres, where the merry fellows had kept him dallying long over a bowl of claret. Now he saw plainly that his pursuers were men of quality, and that two of them were singularly finely built, while the third possessed a figure so slim and delicately proportioned that it might well have been the figure of a young girl. But all three were masked as they had been at the tavern—and this fact alone kept the abbé's suspicions alive.

"Sirs," said he, closing his breviary with a sudden snap, "I observe that you wish to speak with me."

"My lord, the Bishop of Blois," began the tallest of the men, while he doffed his plumed hat with a gesture of profound respect, "it is evident that you are a stranger upon the road to Paris—"

The abbé interrupted him with a momentary display of irritation.

"My son," said he, "I pray you address me by my own name and not by that to which I have no title. It is true that the Bishop of Blois is unhappily dead, but under no circumstances is it possible that so unworthy a successor should be found for the See as the humble priest who has lately enjoyed your hospitality. I, gentlemen, am the Abbé Morellet, curé of the village of Yvette, a man with whom the princes of the Church may well concern themselves but little. I go to Paris now to carry my ward Corinne — you may know her as Mademoiselle de Montesson, gentlemen — to a convent of Benedictine nuns at Charenton. And Heaven forbid that I should aspire to such a distinction as you have named."

He spoke with great dignity, being a man accustomed to command in his own little world. His

HOUSE OF THE SCARLET WITCH

manner was that of one who has made an end of the argument; but the three horsemen, who maintained a fine gravity of demeanour during the parley, would not be put off by it; and they now held their horses at the walk while the leader answered the obstinate abbé.

"My Lord Bishop," said he, "I fear that you jest with us. We know you well, and we are concerned to find you abroad here at such an hour. The Church has too few faithful servants that one of the stoutest of her champions should make himself a mark for footpads. Do you forget that you are about to enter the woods of St. Cloud — and that it is sunset?"

The abbé looked surprised.

"Sirs," said he, "I have never ridden to Paris but once before in all my life, and whether this be St. Cloud or another place, I am, indeed, unable to tell you. Yet for any warning or direction you may be pleased to give me, you will find a grateful listener. I am but a simple priest, gentlemen, and I cannot think that any robber would stoop to find a victim so unprofitable. Heaven be my witness that I have an unpleasant duty to perform in the city yonder. Authority, sirs, is a physic which the surgeon may hesitate to employ, until both persuasion and counsel have been administered. Too long have I been patient — the day for that has passed. Even though the king himself were to intercede, my purpose should be delayed no more. To-morrow, gentlemen, all Paris shall hear that the Hôtel Beautreillis is closed, and that its mistress, my ward, is safe within the convent walls at Charenton."

The abbé was emphatic. He brought this pompous speech to a fitting close with a good thwack of the cudgel nicely laid upon the pony's quarters. His two servants, always imitative, laid two sticks smartly upon the backs of their asses, and all began to ride at a good trot towards the park of St. Cloud. As for the three horsemen, they seemed to enjoy the abbé's company immensely; and they kept close at his side, while merry glances passed between them, and the youngest of the three — who had the figure of a girl — bent low, the better to escape observation. Thus they came altogether to the summit of the hill wherefrom they could see the thick woods about the château of St. Cloud with the river Seine flowing like a river of blood in the valley, and Paris herself away in the distance, the sunlight making red blotches of her domes and towers, and shining with a deep crimson from a thousand west-turned windows. Here, the three strangers drew rein, and one of them, who had not spoken before, addressed the abbé in a parting word.

into the woods, — " I have heard it said that you have but to look upon the woman to be for ever blind."

Jean groaned.

"God grant that our master sees her first," said he.

"And worse than that," said the valet, "if you are young and good-looking, she will kiss you upon the forehead, and then you are branded like one who has been sent to the galleys."

Jean signed.

"Saint Denis!" said he, "I knew how it would be. We shall die here, comrade — and for what? Because we follow our master. Is that our duty? I tell you he is no longer himself. Did you hear how yon fellows called him? Be sure of it — they have bewitched him already. I am ready to die for the abbé of Yvette; but a plague upon me if I ride another league for the Lord Bishop of Blois."

He stopped his ass with the word, and François the valet made haste to imitate him. They were at this moment in a glade so deeply bordered by chestnut-trees that you could scarce see a patch of the grey sky above. The moss beneath their feet was soft and yielding, and the asses' feet sunk in it almost to the hocks. The figure of the abbé was scarce to be discerned, although he rode but twenty paces before them. It was a gloomy spot, dark, threatening, lonely. A stag, which leaped up at their coming, set the hearts of the cowardly pair beating like pumps. And just at the supreme moment of their alarm what should they see in the hollow but a great flash of crimson light, which lit up the brake about them until every twig seemed to have been dipped in blood, every tree trunk to be a scarlet phantom conjured up by the ghostly flames! Twice the light flashed, lurid, smoking, terrible — then darkness fell; and from the wood there came a scream of many voices raised in an awful wail, like the wail of departed spirits or of men in their agony.

At the first flashing of the fire, the abbé's pony stood quite still, shivering with fear. Nor was his master in any better plight.

"François," roared the abbé, "Jean! do you not hear me? God help us all — what a thing to see!"

But François and Jean heard nothing. They were even then on their way back to Yvette, at all the speed of which asses are capable. Long the abbé called them in language which the Church might not have approved, but which the occasion and the abbé's fear demanded. When he found at last that he was alone, beads of perspiration stood upon his forehead, and it seemed

HOUSE OF THE SCARLET WITCH

that a hundred spirits were mocking him in the wood.

"Oh," groaned he, "what do I see — where am I — who is it that follows me? That I should have left my home to come to such a place! Heaven help me or I am surely lost."

He beat his pony the more in his fear, and driving the unwilling beast through the thicket only by a generous application of his cudgel, he came at last out upon a sward upon which great trees cast shadows of fantastic shape. The spot was desolate enough for anything; but it was lighter than the copse he had just quitted; and the stars shining brightly in the grey heaven above seemed to cast down a message of courage.

"Come," said the abbé to himself as he wiped the perspiration from his forehead and began to take heart a little, "why do I fear when I have but ten crowns in my pocket? Who would harm the curé of Yvette? — not the footpads of St. Cloud, I am sure. And I do not believe in spirits — certainly they are for hags' tales. What I saw was the fire of some charcoal-burner. No doubt that was it. My men will come up presently, and we will all go on together. I could laugh to remember what a figure I cut."

He did laugh at the remembrance, but it was a poor attempt — hollow and mocking like the thought which bred it. And he began now to be very anxious for the company of his servants, bidding them come forth from the thicket where he believed them still to lie.

"François, Jean!" he bawled, "it is I, your master, who calls you. What do you fear, knaves? Am I not here to protect you? Oh, surely I will lay my cudgel upon your backs to-morrow."

To his amazement, neither Jean nor François answered his appeal; but in the wood behind him there arose again the eerie wail, and now it was long sustained and piercing, like the wail of witches upon the wing.

"Hail to the Lord Bishop of Blois," was the cry, "hail, hail! Whither he goes, there go we — lolalla — lolalla — lolalla!"

The echo fled from wood to wood and grove to grove, until it died away in moaning sighs, afar, at the heart of the forest. When the last note was stilled, the abbé heard a voice, sweet and fresh and young, crying, —

"What shall be done to the Lord Bishop of Blois?"

And from the woods the answer came, —

"He must suffer, he must suffer — lolalla — lolalla — lolalla!"

A loud peal of laughter followed the words, and while the laughter rang, the thicket was lit again

HOUSE OF THE SCARLET WITCH

with the flaming scarlet light. The abbé's heart threatened to stand still when he saw, grouped there upon the green, the strangest company he had ever beheld in all his life. Dressed in scarlet, some like devils, some like dwarfs, some like hideous creatures with horns protruding from their brows, the throng appeared to be led by a woman whose sugar-loaf cap and sweeping crimson skirts answered in all things to the popular pictures of a witch. When the abbé beheld her she rode upon a great black horse, but those around her were mounted upon white ponies; and the whole company galloping out of the wood, presently they surrounded the trembling ecclesiastic and roared until the very woods rang as with demon voices, —

"Long live the Lord Bishop of Blois — lolalla — lolalla!"

It was a strange scene; the torches, which many of the masqueraders had now lighted, casting a lurid glow upon the scarlet dresses and masks and whitened faces of the dwarfs and demons — horrid monsters, who now flocked about the amazed curé of Yvette. He, on his part, knew not whether the whole were a hideous dream, or the perpetration of some masquerade of which he was to be the victim. Possibly deep down in his mind there was born the question — are these human things or spiritual? Even the learned were gross in superstitution in the middle of the eighteenth century; and the excellent abbé was no wiser than other men — perhaps even a little more prone to believe in omens and the unseen than the common citizen. No wonder if the terror of the wood and the dark of the night and the horrid yells of the horned and hoofed company which now swarmed about him contributed to his bewilderment. A hundred possibilities occurred to him while the cries were still ringing in his ears. He had heard of the terrible jests which courtly masqueraders had perpetrated on those who were obnoxious to them. Could he have given offence in high places — or was it true, after all, that the woods of St. Cloud were peopled by spirits and elves and witches, and that he had fallen into their power? He said he would believe no such tale. Rather would he take courage; and if this were a jest of Corinne's, then should two years instead of one be her portion in the convent.

With this resolution to nerve him, he turned of a sudden upon the horde who pressed about him and began to argue with them.

"Sirs," said he, "I have heard much talk of the Lord Bishop of Blois, and I see plainly that you mistake me for him. Know then that I am but a simple priest, the curé of Yvette, sirs, and that I ride to Paris upon an affair of very great importance."

He spoke the words very slowly, but to his as-

HOUSE OF THE SCARLET WITCH

tonishment no one gave any answer. All together, witches, dwarfs, and demons, they began to repeat his explanation in a sort of monotone, the key of which changed note by note until it rose to a discordant, unearthly shriek.

"Sirs," cried they, "we have heard much talk of the Lord Bishop of Blois, and we see plainly that you mistake us for him. Know then that we are but simple priests, the curés of Yvette, and that we ride to Paris upon an affair of very great importance."

The abbé, deafened by the clamour, put his fingers into his ears and began to shiver with fear.

"*Ciel!*" he murmured, "you are all mad."

"*Ciel!*" repeated the scarlet company, "we are all mad."

The sally was roared rather than intoned; and at the end of it, the whole company bent low in their saddles, the men doffing their hats to the terrified abbé, the women blowing kisses to him.

Then the scarlet woman who appeared to be the mistress of the throng, raised her fresh young voice and asked again, —

"What must be done to the Lord Bishop of Blois?"

And for the second time the answer came, —

"He must suffer — he must suffer — lolalla — lolalla — lolalla!"

The abbé was really frightened now. The wailing melancholy of the chaunt, the hideous shapes of the men who rode at his side, the strange, distorted whitened faces, seemed to him to resemble nothing human, nothing known. Minute by minute the conviction crept upon him that here was the scarlet witch of whom the common people spoke in their folk-tales. The more he said to himself " It is a jest," the farther was his mind from accepting that assurance. He shuddered when he remembered that he was alone with jesters so terrible.

" Oh," he moaned at last, " what do you want with me, what would you do with me ? "

" Oh," echoed the crowd with stentorian voice, " what do you want with us, what would you do with us ? "

" Sirs," wailed the abbé, " for pity's sake have done with it and take me where you will. I have but ten crowns upon me, and those you shall find in my pouch. Get them, I pray you, and permit me to go in peace."

A mocking peal of laughter attended this simple confession.

" What shall be done with the ten crowns of the Lord Bishop of Blois ? " asked a great horned goblin who rode upon the smallest of the small white ponies.

The girl with the crimson hat answered,—

"He shall buy a supper at the house of the scarlet witch."

The command moved the company to frenzies of turbulent delight. Before the bewildered abbé could protest or answer, strong hands had clapped a bandage to his eyes, and knotted it so tightly behind his ears that the whole of the strange vision of grotesque and grinning figures was shut instantly from his view. He knew only that his pony was carrying him rapidly through the forest, that the air became fresher as he mounted to the higher places of the park, that he was led it might have been for the space of ten minutes before his beast was stopped and he was lifted gently to the ground. Never once, however, while the procession moved, did the throng cease their unearthly monotone. The chaunt rose ever like a voice of the night, the wail of spirits wandering, or of phantoms at their pleasures. When it stopped at last with a sudden crash, the abbé's pony stopped too. A strong arm encircled his waist; he was lifted from the saddle and bidden to walk,—he knew that he was entering some room in a house,—a gentle hand forced him into a seat, it removed his bandage; the abbé could see again.

By this time the unhappy man was incapable of surprise. The scene in the wood had robbed him of all power of reason. When they stripped him of his bandage, and he was able to look about him, he neither spoke nor wondered. Yet the spectacle was strange enough to have amazed a bolder man. For the abbé sat at that moment in a room draped in scarlet; and more than that, he sat in a high chair before a long table lit pleasingly by the soft light of many wax candles, and so weighed down with plate and exquisite cut glass that the scarlet drapery below was hardly to be seen. As for the company, that also was a scarlet company,— devils, demons, witches; their whitened faces now hidden by crimson masks, their very hair appearing to be of the brightest red. Even the walls were draped in the same glaring colours; while the attendants, some in hideous masks, some garbed like scarlet elves, capped the scheme fittingly. Yet this was the curious thing — no word was spoken, no greeting given. The company sat like mutes. The abbé shuddered again, for he could not altogether suppress the thought that he might be supping with the risen dead.

Such a haunting suggestion was quick to pass. Though a grim foreboding pursued him while he asked himself, "Where will it end, what did they mean when they called me the Lord Bishop of Blois and said that I must suffer?" — the abbé, good man that he was, — and there was none better in France, — was like other men in possessing a healthy appetite. The groaning table put some heart into him. "I have ridden far, and a well boiled capon with a cup of Burgundy will not come amiss to me," he thought. And so, for the first time since he had entered the terrible wood, he permitted himself to hope. "They will let me ride on when supper is done," he assured himself, "and I shall be in Paris, after all, by the last day of the month. It would never do to be delayed over to-morrow, for the king returns to Paris then, and Corinne will see him and cheat me once more. Certainly, I must be in Paris tomorrow. Meanwhile, I will see what sort of a supper it is, for I am very hungry."

One of the servants had set a plate before him now, — a plate upon which was a little silver dish exquisitely garnished and served. So tempting did the morsel look that the good abbé hastened to plunge his fork into it — but at the first mouthful he made an ugly grimace and was unable to withhold an exclamation.

"How now!" cried he, "that is nothing but bread-crumbs!"

He looked round the table appealingly, but no one in the masked company vouchsafed to him an answer. All were busy upon similar dishes, of which they appeared to partake with exceeding relish. Indeed, they had finished their portions before the abbé had recovered from his astonishment; and while he was still looking at them, a lacquey, dressed in crimson, carried in a dish upon which was a smoking fish of great size, and began to serve slices of it — to the abbé first, and afterwards to the other suppers. At the same moment, another attendant filled the abbé's glass — a magnificent glass of the rarest Venetian work — with wine from a crystal goblet, and then did a similar service for the rest of the company. The action reassured the hungry curé. For the second time he plunged a ready fork into the dish before him. "Fish is fish," he said to himself, while he smacked his lips in famished anticipation. The assurance scarce had comforted him when he broke out with a word which was neither ecclesiastical nor abbatorial.

"Name of the devil!" he exclaimed, "but this is bread too."

How it came to be, in what manner the cheat had been contrived, the abbé knew no more than the dead. Yet there was the fish right enough, and a second mouthful convinced him that it was made of nothing but bread.

"Saint John," cried he, sitting back in his chair, "who ever heard of that — a fish made of breadcrumbs — and every one eating of it as though it were a mullet from the king's table! Body of Saint Paul!—they are all mad."

Mad or sane, the scarlet company appeared to enjoy the fish very much. Their heads bent over their plates, the suppers varied their occupation of eating only by the equally pleasant one of taking long draughts from the crystal goblets before them. They did not appear so much as to notice that the abbé was appealing to them. His words, his exclamations, his questions fell alike upon deaf ears. Not a man listened to him, not a woman raised her eyes to watch him. Nor did his anger, which succeeded presently to his hunger, help him at all. That, too, was absolutely unobserved. Had he roared like a bull, the masked company would have remained oblivious of his presence.

"Ho, ho!" said he at last, while he leant back in his chair and raised the goblet in his hand, "a plague upon the table which sets bread-crumbs before a hungry man!"

He put the goblet to his lips and took a long draught from it. The wine, he had said, would at any rate wash the tasteless bread from his mouth — and so he held the cup long. When at length he put it down, there was upon his face the most unclerical grimace that had ever sat there.

"*Maledetto!*" cried he, "but that is water."

He spoke loudly; nor did he look for an answer, being quite assured by this time that he was dreaming, or if he were not, then that he had become the victim of the strangest jest yet played in France. And he was very much surprised when a voice behind him greeted him with the first word he had heard since he entered the room. For the matter of that, the voice was hardly raised before all the suppers leaped to their feet and stood in an attitude of respectful attention.

"And what is the trouble of the Lord Bishop of Blois?" asked the speaker, as he advanced to the abbé's chair.

He was a man slightly above the medium height, and he wore a dress of white velvet, upon which a lace-work of the whitest diamonds glittered. The abbé observed that he was somewhat advanced in years, and that his features were clear-cut and singularly handsome. He was attended now by two pages, who wore trunk-hose of purple and purple cloaks above them; while an officer in the blue uniform of the Corsican legion stood at his heels as though expecting some command.

"Ho, ho," thought the abbé, as he watched the stranger, "here then is the rogue who has played this jest upon me. I will find a word for him at any rate." And so he spoke aloud.

"Sir," said he, "who you may be I do not wish

HOUSE OF THE SCARLET WITCH

to know; but if this be your house, permit me to tell you that I have been the victim of a great liberty."

The stranger feigned astonishment.

"What," cried he, "have you not supped well, 'seigneur?"

"Sir," answered the abbé, "I beseech you that you will not call me ''seigneur,' for to such a title I have no claim. As for your supper — I would not offer it to a dog."

"But surely," cried the other, feigning great astonishment, "that is turbot which you eat, my friend — and do you not hold a cup of the wine of Burgundy in your hand?"

"Monsieur," said the abbé, with hungry dignity, "whoever has told you that has lied. There is nothing but water here."

"Oh, indeed," cried the new-comer; "pray permit me to put it to my lips, 'seigneur. You say that is water? — Saint Louis, I would like to have a cellar full of such water as that!"

He tasted the draught as he spoke, and smacked his lips over it as though it had been a delicious nectar. The abbé, staggered at the action, was silent for some moments; but after a pause he took the cup up in his hands, and did that which was a rare thing for him to do — he lost his temper.

"My son," he asked, "you declare that to be the wine of Burgundy?"

"Most certainly," replied the stranger; "most admirable wine."

"Then I pray you drink it," exclaimed the abbé — and at the invitation he threw the contents of his goblet into the new-comer's face.

It was a deserved retort, perhaps, but the miserable curé, had he foreseen that which was to follow, would have cut off his right hand before he allowed his temper to carry him so far. Scarce was the thing done when a cry of horror burst from the company about the table. Fifty hands were raised as if to strike the cowering priest. Threats, execrations, remonstrances were hurled at him until his head buzzed with the clamour. The stranger alone appeared to be unmoved. He wiped his face with a handkerchief of lace, and then turned to the Corsican at his elbow.

"I am sorry," said he, "but I must ask you to arrest monsieur, the Bishop of Blois. You will take him to his room and keep him there until my pleasure is known."

"Your majesty is obeyed," was the answer.

There was a great silence in the place now; and it lasted while the Corsican stepped forward and bade the quaking priest follow him. As for the abbé, he was like one petrified.

HOUSE OF THE SCARLET WITCH

"Great Heaven!" he moaned, when they led him from the room, "it is the king who speaks. And I have thrown my wine in his face. God help me, for my day has surely come."

All else was forgotten in this; the visions of the night, his purpose in riding to Paris, even the offences of little Corinne, gave place to the tremendous fear which his folly had brought upon him. He saw it all now — mystery no longer perplexed him. The masquerade in the woods, the horrible apparition, the flashing of the crimson fire — what was it all but the work of the jesters at the palace of St. Cloud! They had gone out to seek whom they could devour, and they had lighted upon the curé of Yvette, he said. Then the king — he had heard, of course, of their pastime, and had come to witness its consummation. And thus had the abbé been led to the perpetration of a crime so terrible. Nothing, not even religion, was held as sacred, in that year 1759, as the body of the king. The abbé knew full well that unless mercy were shown to him, he might spend the remaining years of his life in the prison of Fort-l'Évêque or even in the Bastille. Men had come to such a punishment for mere words — but to throw a goblet of wine in his majesty's face! The very memory of his offending compelled him to shudder like one who was already doomed.

But the Corsican officer had led him to a bedroom now; a pretty room lighted by many wax candles, and furnished with all the taste characterising a period so tasteful. It was a large apartment, with a cabinet giving off it — and the abbé observed in this smaller chamber a supper-table decked prettily with lighted candles and flowers. For this, however, he had no appreciating eyes. He felt at the moment as though he could never eat again. Foreboding, real and stern, had set his nerves itching. He began to question his conductor, hoping for some little word of comfort.

"Monsieur," he said with pitiable anxiety, "I beg you tell me — whose house is this and where does it lie?"

"Readily," answered the young officer. "This is the pavilion of Madame Doublet de Persau. The villagers call it the House of the Scarlet Witch. I regret, monseigneur, that your first acquaintance of it should be made so unpropitiously. Saint Denis! who would have thought that his majesty was unknown to you!"

"God help me," answered the abbé, "I never saw him but once, monsieur, and then it was from a bench in the Place Louis Quinze. Oh, surely he will remember that!"

The Corsican shook his head, implying that he doubted.

"My Lord Bishop," said he, "I am but a very humble servant of his majesty, and Heaven forbid that I should anticipate his decision. If you have friends, however, let me beg of you to write to them. It is possible, should their influence be not delayed, that you may yet atone for this offence with a year in the Bastille."

"A year in the Bastille," murmured the abbé, "a year — the Saints help me — a year for a moment's loss of temper! Oh, *mon Dieu*, will you not plead for me, monsieur? I am no Lord Bishop, but only a poor curé, who is friendless and helpless as you see, my son. I conjure you, of your charity be a friend to me."

"How!" cried the soldier, with a wondrous assumption of surprise, "you tell me, my lord, that you are not the Bishop of Blois! Oh, surely, this night's work has robbed you of your memory. Think a little and you will recall the circumstances. Here to-day you were riding to Paris upon the business of your diocese when you fall into the hands of Madame Doublet de Persau's merry fellows, who bring you to this house to supper. The king, learning of the jest, is driven over from the palace to enjoy it, when you, losing your temper, throw a goblet of wine in his majesty's face, and so become my prisoner until your sentence is delivered. I exhort you, my lord, hide none of these things from yourself, but send at once to your friends and conjure them to intercede for you."

There was a wondrous air of honesty about the Corsican's tale; and although the abbé was more perplexed than ever when the soldier had done, he determined to trust him, and to make a last effort to help himself. Indeed, a sudden inspiration seized upon him, and when he spoke his words came quickly and his white cheeks flushed scarlet.

"Monsieur," he said, "I see it all plainly; they have mistaken me for the Lord Bishop of Blois, and so this misfortune has fallen upon me. I have but one friend in Paris, if, indeed, she be in Paris now. I speak of my ward, Corinne de Montesson, who is to be found at the Hôtel Beautreillis in the Rue St. Paul. Could you but convey a word to her of my necessity, I know that it would not be unavailing. Indeed, she is very gentle and loving to all, and never fails to help those who are in adversity. Send to her, I beg of you, and tell her to come to St. Cloud at once. Say that the Abbé Morellet implores her assistance —"

"*Ciel!*" cried the Corsican, "I will tell her no such tale — for why should she come to the help of the Abbé Morellet when it is Monseigneur the Bishop of Blois whom she is to assist?"

"Sir," said the abbé, with humble entreaty, "if you tell her that, I am surely lost."

HOUSE OF THE SCARLET WITCH

"Courage," said the Corsican, "you forget, monseigneur. In a little time your memory will come back to you. I shall send to Paris at once. Meanwhile you will pardon me if I must hold you under lock and key. You heard the king's command, my lord?"

"God help me," cried the abbé, "I heard it too well."

At this the Corsican withdrew and went downstairs to the supper-table. The scarlet masks of the company were all laid aside now, and the suppers no longer ate fish made of bread-crumbs. On the contrary, they were very merry over flagons of rare red wine and goblets of champagne, and trout from the Lake of Geneva, and dishes of carp's tongues and sturgeon and mullet, and legs of venison, and fat capons. When they saw the officer, they cried out joyfully, and hastened to ask how the abbé did.

"Grimod, Grimod, what does he say, what does he do — oh, tell us quickly — we die with impatience — you have news, Grimod?"

The Corsican held up his hand for quiet. Then, addressing the scarlet witch, — whose fresh and piquant face belied her rôle now that the mask was laid aside, — he said, —

"*Ma foi!* Mademoiselle Corinne, the abbé asks for you."

"For me?" said the girl; "then you have told him, Grimod?"

"Upon my word, mademoiselle, I have told him nothing. He thinks you are at the Hôtel Beautreillis, and he begs me to send a messenger there."

Corinne clapped her pretty hands.

"Oh," she said, "how I love him! But he will not send me to a convent after all."

The idea that Corinne de Montesson would ever succumb to such a fate seemed to amuse the masqueraders very much. They greeted her words with extravagant enthusiasm. One love-sick swain — whose devil's head was set mockingly upon a plate before him — turned toward her, eyes full of sheepish affection, and exclaimed, —

"Saint John, Corinne, if you go to the nuns at Charenton, you will take half Paris with you."

"We shall have to build a city there," cried another.

"Such a place of worship will never have been seen," said a third.

"I go as maid-in-waiting," lisped a pretty boy, who was busy with a dish of venison.

"And the king, what does he go as?" asked a demon, whose head was tucked away under his chair.

HOUSE OF THE SCARLET WITCH

"Yes," cried Corinne, joyfully, "the king, where is he? Come forth, sir, and let us see you."

"*Sacrebleu!*" answered a voice from the further end of the table, "the king is very well, thank you, mademoiselle — but he will be the better when he has eaten this pasty."

Could the abbé have seen the king at that moment his fears would have vanished like the wind. Truth to tell, his majesty looked exceedingly unkingly, seated as he was astride a small chair and holding a very large pasty between his knees. But the wretched priest in the bedroom above knew of none of these things. While the masqueraders below were at the zenith of their merriment, the miserable abbé was pacing his elegant prison; and every turn he took brought a fresh exclamation to his lips.

"Oh," he would moan, "a year in the Bastille at the least — that I should have left my home for this! A year in the Bastille, where they put you in cages so that your bones are bent; or in ditches, where the floors are deep in slime! Heaven be merciful to me — I have thrown wine in the king's face! Fool that I was! — his dress should have taught me better manners. And now they will punish me — oh, miserable day, unhappy hour — what would I not give to be in my bed at Yvette again!"

He, good man, had lived so noble a life that fear had not in all his years been an enemy to him. But now he feared exceedingly, — feared so that for a long while he started at every whisper of the wind or creak of board; feared until he forgot that he was hungry and had not supped. By and by, however, one of his restless pacings carried him into the cabinet which opened off the bed-chamber; and then he beheld the little table with the flowers and the wax-lights and the flagon of red wine and the well-dressed capon.

"Bah!" he exclaimed angrily, "the wine is but coloured water, the capon is made of bread — they shall not befool me a second time."

He thought it a cruel jest, and vowed he would not be the victim of it; and so he began to pace the room again; but his steps carried him, despite his resolution, straight into the cabinet again; and at the third time of his coming, hunger and thirst so far prevailed that he poured a little of the wine from the flagon and ventured to taste it.

"Oh," cried he, filling a goblet to the brim, "can it be true? — upon my word, this is very like the wine of Burgundy — Saint John! I have never tasted a better imitation."

There was almost a smile upon the abbé's face now, and he began with eager hands to

HOUSE OF THE SCARLET WITCH

help himself to the capon. A moment later he had seated himself at the little table and was busy with a groaning plate. Only when the meal was done did a haunting memory of his night's work come back to him — and at that, the wine was soured and the bread turned bitter. He looked at the great carved bed, and told himself that sleep was not for such as him. He heard a bell without strike the hour of midnight, and the new-come day seemed to be the herald of his misfortunes. Once or twice he went to the door of his prison-chamber and listened, but could distinguish no sound, neither of voices nor of steps.

"Holy Saints!" cried he, beginning to pace his room again, "if I could only lie this night in my bed at Yvette!"

He sighed at the hopelessness of the desire; but, to his intense amazement, his sigh was echoed from the opposite side of the room. And he was very surprised when, upon turning round, he beheld, standing there by a picture let into the panel of the wainscoting, two of the masked men who had met him on the road earlier in the evening. Indeed, the abbé rubbed his eyes to make sure that he did not dream; and it was not until the tallest of the two spoke that he believed altogether in the reality of that which he saw.

"My Lord Bishop," said the stranger, "we

have kept our promise, and you see us again. Is it gladly?"

"Gentlemen," cried the abbé, "gladly indeed — oh, Heaven knows! You have heard of my misfortune?"

The masked man raised his hand.

"Hush," said he; "a word may cost you your life. We know all, and have come to save you. Follow me, 'seigneur, and say nothing, whatever you may see or hear."

With this, he laid his hand upon a button in the picture, and the panel slid back noiselessly, showing a narrow aperture through which the three men passed — and then, the dazed abbé! The aperture thus disclosed gave access to a narrow flight of stairs, at the foot of which was a little door opening at the back of the pavilion directly upon the park of St. Cloud. Before the abbé had realised anything of that which was being done, he found himself out upon the soft grass with the bridle rein of a horse in his left hand and a groom at his right hand waiting to assist him to mount. The two men in their turn went to horses waiting for them, and all leaping into the saddles, the leader said presently, —

"'Seigneur, mount, I beg of you. We ride to Blois for your life."

"To Blois?" gasped the abbé.

HOUSE OF THE SCARLET WITCH

But the groom had helped him into the saddle now, and the man having sent the horse off to join the others with a lusty smack upon the quarters, the abbé found himself, for good or ill, galloping wildly through the park towards the road for Sèvres. So absorbed was he in doubt and wonder that he failed to observe that a young girl now rode with his guides — though she was masked as the others were. Indeed, those with him never drew rein nor spoke a single word until dawn broke in the sky and St. Cloud and its woods lay far behind them. Then for the first time they permitted their foaming beasts to go at the walk and the fresh wind of the morning to breathe upon their heated faces.

The place was the summit of a hill some five miles from the town of Rambouillet. Below them a valley stretched pleasantly, and in the far distance the spire of the church at Yvette stood up like a needle against the cloudless sky.

"My lord," said the leader of the strangers as he halted suddenly at the spot, "yonder is your home. As for us, our work is done. We have but to give you this paper and to bid you make your way to Blois with all speed. I doubt not that you will obey faithfully the king's wish that you shall not leave your new diocese for the space of one year."

"My diocese — the king's wish!" exclaimed the abbé, whose face was bathed with perspiration and whose limbs were so sore that he could scarce sit upon his horse.

"Certainly," answered the masked man, pressing the paper into the priest's hands; "read that and all will be known to you."

The abbé read the paper; then he raised his hands in an attitude of humble thankfulness.

"Merciful Heaven be praised," cried he, "they have made me Bishop of Blois, me — the unworthy — the simple priest — the humble curé of Yvette! Surely the king has forgiven me then. Gentlemen, I thank you from my heart for this night's work. Never shall your services be forgotten. Tell me your names, I beg of you, that I may remember them in my prayers."

The first of the men removed his mask.

"'Seigneur," said he, "they call me Bénoît, the swordsman."

"'Seigneur," cried the second, unmasking in his turn, "I am the Comte de Guibert — the oldest friend of your ward, Mademoiselle Corinne de Montesson."

It was the moment for the young girl now. Swiftly unmasking and turning her pretty face upon the astonished abbé, she said, —

"And I, 'seigneur, am Corinne herself."

The abbé sat as one dumfounded. Tears welled up in his eyes. Gratitude choked his words.

"Corinne," he said, " oh, it is to you that I owe my pardon and my fortune then! God bless you a thousand times."

"But not at Charenton," cried Corinne, merrily.

"Heaven forbid," cried the abbé. "Return to your home and carry an old man's blessing with you."

. . . . .

The Bishop of Blois was wont to tell, even in his old age, how that at St. Cloud he had once thrown a glass of wine in the king's face. But the knowing ones shook their heads.

"Bah!" said they among themselves, " it was one of pretty Corinne's jests. The only king our good bishop ever met was Lekain, the actor from the king's theatre."

THE PURPLE GLASS

V

THE PURPLE GLASS

The Chevalier Eugène Sabatier was accounted one of the handsomest rogues in all Paris; but he looked neither handsome nor roguish when he stood in the music-room of the Hôtel Beautreillis on the third day of May in the year 1763, and reflected earnestly upon the strange tale which Antonio, the physician, had just told him.

The glorious afternoon was coming to a close then, and the old gardens in the Rue St. Paul began to be filled with the first sweetness of the night. Trees laden with blossoms, bushes with roses, rustled gently as the warm south wind breathed upon them; lengthening shadows upon the grass waged war with the delaying patches of sunlight and drove them inch by inch from the garden. The spires and turrets of the great house shone radiant a little while with fiery beams which struck upon their windows and copper domes and made them like burning beacons above the surrounding streets. In the music-room itself, a soft twilight prevailed; and this was in keeping with the gloom which had come upon those in the chamber.

There were three persons in the great room at that hour; but the young chevalier was the most prominent figure, standing as he did where the deep red light of the setting sun could strike upon the gold and blue of his dragoon's uniform, and even send fire flashing from the heavy brass helmet he held in his hand. As for Mademoiselle Corinne, the mistress of the Hôtel Beautreillis, she sat in a low chair drawn so far behind the curtain of the window that her pretty face was all in a shadow; nor could you distinguish the colour of her robe nor the tint of the lace which hid her exquisitely white neck. But it was plain that she was very serious; and the same might have been said of her old physician Antonio, who sat at a great writing table in the centre of the apartment, and dipped his long quill pen into the ink-horn before him with irritating regularity. Never once did he look at the young officer, nor seem to remember the astonishment which a word of his had just created. And this was the more surprising since that word had told of the officer's death.

"Monsieur," he had said, "if you go to the Château Saint Mandé to-night, you go to the house of a man who is waiting to kill you."

The chevalier sprang from his chair, and standing a moment with the crimson light flashing upon his young face, he appeared like one about to resent a savage insult.

"*Dieu !*" cried he, "do you forget that I am going to the house of my brother?"

"I forget nothing," answered the old man, without looking up from his paper. "Should you doubt my words, monsieur, it is easy to prove them by continuing your journey immediately to the château. But the proof will be with us — for your body will lie in the Marne before midnight."

The prophecy was that of one who weighed his words well; but so terrible was it to hear, that long minutes passed and no voice broke the silence in the music-room. As for Eugène Sabatier, he might have been stricken dumb. Doubt, dread, anger, fear — each of these played upon his boyish face in their turn. Saying to himself at one moment that the story was a hideous calumny, in the next he remembered the untold wrongs he had suffered at his brother's hand, and a voice whispered in his ear, "The physician is right." Corinne, meanwhile, watched her guest with sad eyes and a troubled mind. There was something beyond mere friendship in a glance like that. Had her thoughts been uttered aloud, she would have said, "I love him." Happily for her, the curtain hid her face, and the pretty flush which added ornament to it. When she spoke, there was scarce a ring of tenderness in her voice.

"Eugène," she said, for they had been children together, and no formalities stood between them, — "Eugène, do not think that Antonio would jest with you at such a moment. This is no new thing to him. He has known your brother, the Count of Brives, for twenty years. I sent for you to-night to save your life — repay me by forgetting everything but the fortune and the future which to-night may bring you."

The young soldier, distracted by a hundred thoughts, turned upon her a glance full of affection yet hardly followed her words.

"Corinne," cried he, "I know that my brother hates me — yet, that he would kill me — *mon Dieu*, I cannot believe that."

"Nevertheless," chimed in the old physician, "he killed your brother Gilbert."

An exclamation almost of resentment broke from Sabatier.

"Monsieur," he gasped, "you say — ?"

"That your brother Gilbert was poisoned by the Count of Brives in the Château Saint Mandé two years ago to-night."

"Oh," exclaimed Sabatier, sinking into a seat and burying his face in his hands, "God grant that you are wrong!"

"Antonio is never wrong," said Corinne, sadly. "If you ask him, he will tell you that your brother was poisoned three weeks after he became marshal of the palace — an appointment the Count of Brives had applied for but had failed to obtain."

"In the same way that you, monsieur," added Antonio, "having been ordered to Westphalia to supplant the count in a command there, will be poisoned by him on the eve of your departure."

The old man spoke with such deliberate emphasis and conviction, his story was so plausible, that Sabatier could suffer it no longer.

"Corinne," cried he, rising from his seat and suppressing the many emotions which rushed upon his brain, "it is all like a terrible dream to me. I must go home to reason with it. And if it be as you say, then I thank God that my brother is saved from this new crime."

He held out his hand to her; but she did not take it.

"Eugène," she exclaimed, "before you go home to-night you have work to do."

"Which is, Corinne?"

"To avenge your brother Gilbert and to become the Count of Brives."

Perplexed as he was, Sabatier smiled.

"Oh," said he, "now you speak to me in

riddles. What miracle shall make me Count of Brives to-night?"

"Supper at the Château Saint Mandé is the only miracle necessary, Eugène."

The young man drew back with an impatient gesture.

"Corinne," he cried, "is it an hour for jests?"

"I do not jest with you, Eugène," she answered very tenderly. "Did not I tell you that fortune and a future awaited you to-night? It is for you to say whether you will take the gift or refuse it."

She spoke very simply, though deep feeling gave a quaver to her voice. As for Sabatier, he began to tell himself that he had lost his wits; and he walked up and down the room like a man distracted.

"Come," cried he, stopping suddenly at last; "what mystery is this? You say that my brother will poison me, yet you tell me to sup with him. I beseech you be plain with me — oh, do I not suffer enough that you should add to my burden?"

He turned from one to the other appealingly, his distress being so great that tears stood in his eyes, and his voice was husky and broken. But it was the old physician who answered him.

"Monsieur," said he, laying down his pen for

the first time, "you beseech me to be plain with you, and I will hasten to obey your wish. Mademoiselle tells you truly that fortune and a future await you at the Château Saint Mandé to-night; but if they are to be won, they will be won by your own courage. The Count of Brives asks you to his home that he may kill you as he killed your brother Gilbert. If you turn back now, thinking to spare him the crime, you will dishonour your father's memory and add new shame to a house which knew shame for the first time when your eldest brother was born to it. Let me conjure you, then, to do no such thing, but to ride hence at once for the Château — "

"Where they will poison me?" interrupted Sabatier, a little angrily.

"Exactly," continued Antonio, "where they will poison you. But you, if you are careful to do exactly as I bid you, you will awake presently from the death you shall seem to die, and being awakened, will find yourself in twenty hours Count of Brives and master of his fortune."

Sabatier stood wonder-struck. The old man, excited now by the story he was telling, raised his hand as in warning, and continued rapidly, —

"Monsieur, there is no other in the world who is called, as you are now called, to be God's messenger in this work of vengeance and of right.

Go, then, before the clock strikes again, to Saint Mandé; and say to yourself as you enter, 'I am come to avenge my brother Gilbert.' Whatever you see there, whatever may happen to you — fear nothing. The eyes of those that send you to this work will watch you even as you sit. I say no more — the minutes pass swiftly; and what further counsel I can give is written here upon this parchment. Let me exhort you to read every letter of that injunction — not once, but twelve times, as you ride toward the château. For that writing is life or death — as you remember or forget it."

There was a great stillness in the room when the old man ceased to speak. Sabatier, scarce knowing whether the words were real or the echo of a dream, took with trembling hands the paper which the physician thrust upon him. Then he turned questioningly to Corinne; but she had now risen from her seat, and coming forward she laid her pretty fingers caressingly upon his arm.

"Eugène," she asked earnestly, "you will avenge your brother?"

"As God is my witness," he answered, "I will know the truth this night."

The woods of Vincennes were very dark when Eugène Sabatier passed through them on his way to his brother's house. But his head was too full of terrible thoughts to permit him to notice the state of the night or even the dangers of the road. For the matter of that he had ridden at a hand-gallop from Mademoiselle Corinne's courtyard; and skirting the right bank of the Seine, he drew rein but twice before the grim and forbidding home of the Count of Brives stood up in the valley before him. Then, indeed, with a little shiver of fear he permitted his horse to walk, while he took off his heavy brass helmet and wiped the sweat from his forehead.

"*Ciel!*" he said to himself, "what an errand to go upon! That my brother should be a poisoner. Bah, I will not believe it! Corinne has been too clever for once. That old fool of a physician has deceived her with his nonsense. As well might I expect to be Pope as to step into Charles's shoes and become Count of Brives to-morrow. Yet I cannot forget that poor Gilbert's body was found in the river the morning after he supped at Saint Mandé. God help me — what am I to think?"

He was riding at that moment through a wood of shivering aspens; and what with the strange, haunting music of their leaves, and the darkness of the thicket, and the weird light playing upon the river, whose course he could mark, like a great silver vein of the valley, he began to be more fearful than ever he had been in all his life. And this was surprising, since there was no braver man in Condé's legion than Eugène Sabatier; none readier with the rapier, or more skilled in all those arts which are a soldier's boast. It was the hidden danger — the death in the cup — that now made his heart beat so loudly. He could not hide it from himself that this old man, who had warned him, might be a fool and a boaster. How, he asked himself, if the scheme should fail and his own body be found to-morrow in the Marne? He had little to hope for in life, for he was a penniless soldier, who must make his own future; but so long as he could treasure up in his heart love for little Corinne, he was content to live, and to dream of a day when there should be no gulf of wealth and station between them. That day would come quickly enough if his brother, the Count of Brives, were to die, since the count had neither wife nor child; and title and lands would then descend to him. He remembered that Corinne had promised that all this should happen twenty hours after he had sat down to supper at the château; and he laughed again at the absurdity of her promise. Only when he remembered poor Gilbert did his own courage come back to him; and riding quickly out of the wood he swore that the truth should be hidden no longer.

THE PURPLE GLASS

He was not more than a hundred yards from the gloomy house now; and he could hear the voices of boatmen rising up from the river's bank. Behind him lay Paris, her lights beginning to shine brightly as in joy of the newly come night; before him the road sloped gently toward the Seine, meeting it at last at a point where the Marne flows into the greater stream. He could see his brother's château, which had the shape of an old-time fortress, standing up black and threatening almost at the water's edge. In the distance it appeared to be the stronghold of the hamlet which lay in its shadow; a hamlet of tumbling cottages, with an old Norman church, red-roofed, squat, yet withal picturesque. But when you rode into the one street of this village, you observed that a meadow lay between the great house and its humbler children; and that the former was girded about with a wood of poplars. Indeed, it was a very lonely house, and all the villagers shunned it, as they shunned its melancholy, silent, solitude-loving master, the Count Charles of Brives.

These villagers were all going to their beds when the young captain of Condé's legion rode at a canter through their hamlet. He, on his part, took little notice of them or of their dwellings, so entirely did apprehension of the peril to come play upon his mind. Twice already had he perused the slip of parchment which old Antonio intrusted to him with so solemn a warning; but now, at the mouth of the village, he drew rein for the third time, and holding the paper so that the light from the lantern of the inn fell upon it, he read every word of it again and again; and having read it, he repeated it twenty times aloud, to be sure that his memory had it. There were but three lines of writing in all — done clearly, in great bold characters; and Eugène soon knew them so well that he could say them backwards or forwards as he pleased: —

BEWARE OF THE PURPLE GLASS
THE HALF OF THAT WITHIN IT IS LIFE
THE WHOLE IS DEATH.

"Bah!" said he, tearing the paper into shreds and letting the night wind scatter it, "they tell a tale to frighten children — not men. What an injustice to believe this of my brother until I have something beyond an old man's cackle to go upon. How should he know of a purple glass, and how can there be both life and death within it? I will listen to no such slander, but sup with the count as brother should."

This was all very well in promise, but the performance was a different matter. Though Sabatier kept telling himself that he had nothing to fear, his heart beat wildly when ultimately he stood at the gate of the château and heard the great bell booming in the tower above him. What, he asked, if that gate, which now shut behind him with such an ominous clang, should never open to his knock again! How if the morn should find his body lapped upon by the waters yonder, sedge grass hiding his face, and the reeds trying vainly to clothe him with warmth! He could not suppress a shudder when a voice whispered in his ear — "All this is possible." Nor did the croaking welcome of the evil-eyed, stooping, lank old servant, Armand, reassure him.

"The count, my master, awaits you in the salon, monsieur," said he. "I pray you be careful of the steps — they are, like all else here, a little grown in age. Shall Germain bed your horse, or do you ride away to-night?"

"Ay, surely, Armand; I leave Paris to-morrow, and must be in my own bed before midnight is struck," answered Eugène, merrily — though his heart sank lower and lower at the gloomy aspect of all he saw about him. "Let the horse have a mouthful of sweet hay and a loosened girth," he added presently; "who knows that my hand will be steady enough to saddle him when I have done supping with the count!"

The old servant, who had thrown the reins to

the lad Germain, looked up quickly at this remark, his toothless mouth opening in a horrid smile.

"Who knows, monsieur?" he said; "there was never one of your race that refused a flask of Armagnac yet. And there is none better in France than the wine in my master's cellars. I pray you follow me lest the supper be already cold."

With this, he took up his lantern and mounted a steep, tortuous narrow staircase, above which the great black walls of the château loomed forbiddingly. There was a wicket in an old iron-sheathed door at the stair's head, and when they had passed through it, they stood in a vast hall, the walls of which were covered with rusting armour. But the place was forsaken and unlighted, save for the poor rays which fell from the candle in the lantern; and, indeed, the whole house was full of a silence as of the silence of death. It was a tremendous relief to Eugène when at last he entered the great salon and beheld his brother standing near the door to receive him. Every suspicion, every doubt, all the horrid stories he had heard at the Hôtel Beautreillis, were forgotten in a moment. Kinship, even affection, succeeded to them during the instant of warm welcome.

"Brother," he said, coming forward with a light step, and stooping to kiss the count upon the cheeks, — " brother, it is good to see you again."

THE PURPLE GLASS

Count Charles suffered rather than returned the greeting. He was a man perhaps of forty years of age: his face pitted with the small-pox; his nose squat and up-turned; his beard short and stubby; his eyes very bright and very small. He wore a suit of black velvet with ruffles of white lace; but his vest was embroidered with silver, and the buttons of it were picked out with diamonds.

"My brother," said he, his restless eyes blinking the while, "I heard that you were named for a command in Westphalia. It was natural that I should wish to see you before you go."

It sounded almost like an apology; but Eugène, refusing to notice the hesitation and halting manner, became frankness itself.

"It is true," he answered, "that I have a command, Charles — though there is little hope left to us of the war. I am sure you wish me God-speed, for I am to have your old company in Condé's legion."

The count shrugged his shoulders.

"Pah!" said he, curtly, "if you can make those rats fight, you are a clever man. They ran at Minden like deer from the dogs. Let us sit to supper and forget them."

He led the way to an adjoining dining-room, even a larger chamber than the one they quitted; and they sat together at the end of a long table, feebly lit by eight wax lights. The toothless old man, Armand, waited upon them, like a ghostly image from the gloom in which the greater part of the room was plunged. For a while, neither of the brothers spoke a word, eating silently and scarce looking at one another. The supper itself was of the plainest — a capon, a dish of spinach, some tender slices of venison — and for drink, champagne in long goblets of sparkling cut glass. Eugène said to himself for the second time when he lifted such a goblet and drank deeply of the foaming draught, that old Antonio, the physician to Mademoiselle Corinne, was a fool. There was no such thing as a purple glass upon the table. How, then, could he avoid that within it? They had told him a hag's tale. Surely it was one of pretty Corinne's jests. For a truth, he was half of a mind to hint to his brother the cruel slander put abroad about him; but restraining himself, he began to talk of the Hôtel Beautreillis and of its fascinating mistress.

"You have seen Corinne lately?" he asked indifferently.

. The count looked up quickly.

"You speak of Mademoiselle de Montesson?" said he.

"Certainly I do; but I thought you were such good friends."

THE PURPLE GLASS

Count Charles shrugged his shoulders.

"I know her a little," said he, with assumed nonchalance, "and you —"

"Oh," said Eugène, with whole-hearted energy, "I know her very well indeed, brother."

The count put out his glass that Armand might fill it with champagne. The action helped him to conceal from Eugène the deep flush upon his face, and the angry brightness of his eyes. But he said no word to betray himself, and began cleverly to talk of other subjects with a loquacity quite foreign to him. As for the younger man, though he was quite content now to believe that Corinne had told him a silly story, none the less did the influence of his surroundings weigh heavily upon him. His heart was dark as the great room in which he sat; and just as in that chamber eight candles cast an aureole of light at its centre, so in his own heart was there a glow of light when he remembered his love for pretty Corinne. "Shall I ever see her again?" he asked. A relentless foreboding warned him that he might not. Danger seemed all about him. He knew that his brother hated him — hated him because his mother had loved him; hated him for his looks, his friends, his successes. But he knew then that he hated him most of all because of the word which he had spoken about little Corinne.

Supper was done now; and the count, pushing back his chair from the table, seemed to be in a more generous mood.

"Armand," he cried to the toothless old serving man, "bring a flask of Armagnac and set glasses. You can go to the lodge then."

Eugène was surprised at the request.

"Do you live here alone, brother?" he asked.

"Certainly," replied the count; "am I not a soldier who has been alone all my life?"

It was a bitter question, and Eugène shuddered — he knew not why. Far from fearing his brother now, he pitied him, and would have been very glad to say so; but just when the word was upon his lips, Armand returned with the flask of the wine of Armagnac and two long glasses, which he wiped and set carefully upon the table. Eugène observed their colour immediately. They were of a deep purple tint. "*Ciel!*" he murmured to himself, while his heart beat fast and the blood rushed to his brain, "*the purple glass.*" In the same instant, Armand left the room; and a little while after a gate in the courtyard was shut with a loud clang. The brothers were alone in the house of gloom.

The count was the first to speak. He had the flask of wine in his hand; and Eugène, who watched him like one fascinated, observed that his arm trembled when he raised it.

THE PURPLE GLASS

"Come," said he, in a thick, unnatural voice, "there is no finer Armagnac in Paris than this. Let me give you some."

Eugène bowed his head. His face was almost livid now. For that which he must suffer, he cared nothing. He would sooner have died there and then than make sure of so horrible a truth. "My brother a poisoner," he said to himself a a hundred times, " oh, what shame, what dishonour!"

The count filled his glass and pushed it over to him. Eugène was surprised to see that his brother helped himself also to the wine, drinking the half of a glass at a draught. The action reassured him. "They have told me a lie," he said to himself for the twentieth time — and with this upon his lips and the warning of old Antonio ringing in his ears like a knell, he lifted the purple glass and drank from it. "The half is life," said the voice. Eugene drank exactly one half and put the glass upon the table. The count did not appear to notice the action.

"So you leave Paris to-morrow?" said he, pleasantly.

The dragoon answered incoherently. A strange joy began to quicken the blood in his veins. He had looked to fall senseless after drinking the wine, but to his amazement nothing happened. Rather he felt elated, eager to talk nonsense, light-headed as a child. "Pish," said he to himself, "what a calumny to spread!" The reaction was terrible, overwhelming. He had the desire to rise and embrace his brother. He spoke of little Corinne freely — even of his love for her. The count replied in monosyllables. He, too, was watching, but the light of long years of hate was in his eyes. The moment of his vengeance had come, he said.

Five minutes had passed now since Eugène drank the wine; five minutes which he declared were the happiest in his life. But, of a sudden, his joy was turned to great fear; his words were broken on his lips; cold sweat started to his forehead; his heart quickened with a pulse of weakness. In that instant he knew that the old physician had not cheated him. Death himself seemed to have touched him upon the forehead. A dreamy, irresistible sleep stole upon him, surely. Everything in the room was still clear to his eyes; but the power of action and of speech was becoming less every moment. He felt that he was sinking down into unconsciousness. "Oh," he moaned, "I shall never see little Corinne again." All his love for her was magnified a thousand times at the thought. He clenched his hands and swore that he would not die. With a last effort, and a last loud cry, he raised himself from his chair — only to fall headlong at his brother's feet; and to lie there, seeing all, hearing all, but unable to move a limb or utter a word.

The Count of Brives, who had waited for the moment, rose for the first time since his brother had drunk the wine. Eugène, lying there in the trance which the poison put upon him, could observe all the other's actions — and he watched him as a prisoner may watch a captor from whom he has no hope of mercy. Deliberately and with all the nerve of a man grown callous to crime, the count began to finish his work. He put out the lights upon the table one by one, until a single candle alone lighted the vast chamber. Then, taking this candle in his hand, he bent over the body before him and looked at it with a malignity woeful to see.

"Pah!" he said, placing the light upon the table again, "Condé's legion will want a captain to-morrow, and Corinne a lover. He brought it upon himself — why should I pity him?"

The dragoon heard the words very plainly, and the hate in them added to that which he suffered. It was true, then, as Antonio had told him, that his brother meant to kill him when he asked him to the Château Saint Mandé. He recollected at the same time that the old man had prophesied things which he did not understand at the moment of their utterance. "You will awake presently from the death you shall seem to die, and being awakened, will find yourself in twenty hours Count of Brives and master of his fortunes." Or again: "The eyes of those that send you to this work will watch you even as you lie." Would he, indeed, he asked himself, wake again from this paralysis which had fallen upon heart and tongue and limb? Did some friendly eyes indeed watch him as he lay there in all the agony of a trance? He could not answer; could do nothing but think of little Corinne and pray that he might see her once again.

The Count of Brives had opened the window of the salon now, and the cool air of the May night flooded the chamber refreshingly. Eugène heard his brother pass out into the garden beyond, and when he returned to the table he had a lantern in his hand. Nerved by all the resolution of daring and cruelty, he was quick to act, that his crime might be hidden from men and from his own eyes. Ever and anon Eugène could observe his pale face as he moved swiftly about the room, or listened with strained ear to catch any sound in the house. But the silence of ultimate night reigned in the château. No human thing moved there. Not a clock ticked, not a door creaked. The wind moaned its song of solitude in the poplars of the garden — but the count was alone with his victim.

THE PURPLE GLASS

Twice he walked up to the body of the man he believed to be dead; twice he drew back with a tremor of nerve and a gesture of repugnance. When at last his iron will conquered, he stooped quickly, and bringing all his great strength to the work, he began to drag the body toward the window. It was a horrid effort even for him; and he had but begun it when a loud sound, like the sound of a door shutting in a chamber above, caused him to spring up with a great cry, and to stagger from the room as though unnumbered phantoms had come about him to proclaim the deed. Eugene heard the sound well enough, and began to hope for the second time. "They watch me, they watch me!" he cried, — "oh, how I need my courage! — if they should be too late!" The thought was unbearable, almost maddening; the agony of the bondage of helplessness greater than any man could conceive. He prayed for unconsciousness, even for death — but these were denied to him. The drug had quickened his life — and yet had robbed him of all that which life is.

In this the mood of fear unspeakable, he lay and listened while his brother passed quickly from room to room, opening and shutting the doors loudly, and often crying "Who goes there?" as though he was sure that some one else had entered the château. Nor was the count content until he had searched even the garrets, and had told himself a hundred times that the wind cheated him in his alarm. When at last he returned to the dining-room, his step was stronger and his will more sure. He picked up the body now as though it had been a common burden, and staggering from step to step down the stairs upon which the window opened, he dragged it into the garden, and so out into the moonlight, which fell plenteously upon the damp grass. There for a moment he stood panting for his breath and shading his eyes, that he might see more clearly into the garden. As for Eugène, he had felt the strength of the arms which clasped him so surely; and now when he lay stiff and voiceless upon the grass, he said that death had become his neighbour. " He means to throw my body in the Seine," he thought; " they will come too late — they have left me to die — what cruelty! — what a night of suffering!" Had a voice then been given to him, he would have screamed in his terror. But the drug had tied his tongue; the trance held him too surely — he was dead, yet suffered as the living rarely have suffered.

Once more the count stooped to his dreadful work. The spot whereon he stood was scarce a hundred yards from the black waters of the Seine. There was to be no delay this time. Turning his

HE PICKED UP THE BODY AND STAGGERED DOWN.

eyes away that he might not look upon his brother's face again, he gripped him by the left arm and began to drag him toward the river. Two paces he took; his foot was raised for a third — when the second omen of the night sent him staggering back from his burden like one stricken with a mortal sickness. The omen was nothing less than the sound of his name uttered from a window high up in the looming wall of the château. Clear above the river's moaning and the song of the poplars, the call came: —

"Monsieur le Comte, Monsieur le Comte, where is your brother Eugène?"

The count turned round on his heel — a cry frothed upon his lips — he reeled backward, backward, saying that the judgment of God was upon him. The château, which had been dark when he left it five minutes before, was now blazing with light. Every room on the upper story shed bright golden rays from its windows. Seen in the strong moonlight, the great house had become like a palace of the fairies. The panes of glass were so many stars shining in a setting of black stone; the very attics were beacons to guide those far away in the valley. More than all, a man clothed from head to foot in black stood plain to be seen at a casement above the salon; and he it was who called to Count Charles, —

"Monsieur le Comte, Monsieur le Comte, where is your brother Eugène?"

The count heard the call, and for a moment terror convulsed him. But fury was quick to prevail above fear; and with a great oath upon his lips, he drew a dagger and ran back to the château. In the same instant, the man in black disappeared from the window; and Eugène, watching it all with a hope not to be described, observed that the bushes near to him on the lawn opened suddenly, and that men came out of them. The face of the first of these new-comers was hidden by a mask; but when the man stooped presently to pour the contents of a phial upon the dragoon's lips, the mask slipped and Eugène knew that old Antonio was at his side.

"My son," said the old man, watching the red drops fall upon the feverish lips, "awake — and sleep."

"*Ciel!* is it thou, Antonio?" murmured Eugène, knowing that the trance had passed from him the moment the drops fell, "Oh, blessed be God — I live — I live!"

That minute was the most exquisite of his life; but scarce had he realised the meaning of it when a sweet unconsciousness stole upon him, and he slept. And so sleeping, the men raised him in their arms and carried him quickly out of the garden.

THE PURPLE GLASS

The afternoon of the following day was drawing to its close when Eugène Sabatier awoke from his deep sleep. A ray of burning sunlight striking down through the open window of his room in the Rue Charles V., fell at length upon his eyes, and caused him to turn uneasily upon his bed. A moment later, he sat upright and began to stare about him with the air of one who is not quite sure either of the hour or of his environment. In which operation, he encountered the gaze of his servant Barnardin, who stood at the bed's head as though he had long been awaiting the moment.

"Sir," said the valet, advancing with his master's clothes, "it is five o'clock, and you know that we leave Paris at eight. Will you be pleased to rise?"

"*Diavolo!*" cried Eugène, springing from the bed with a light step — and he was very much surprised to find how strong he was — "have I slept long, Barnardin?"

Barnardin shook his head.

"You were away from home when I left here at ten o'clock last night, my master," said he; "but when I brought your coffee at eight o'clock this morning you slept so soundly that I could not wake you."

The dragoon began to dress himself quickly, remembering only that he had orders to leave Paris at eight o'clock that night.

"*Sang-bleu!*" muttered he to himself, "I must have supped in some cabaret — and drunk too much Armagnac. What a thing to dream — that my brother poisoned me! Pah! it was a fool's sleep, and I am paid for my folly. And yet I could swear that I talked with Corinne at her house yesterday, and that she promised to make me Count of Brives in twenty hours. *Dame!* I am like to wait long for that!"

The reflection made him a little gloomy, reminding him as it did how small had been fortune's gifts to him, and how childish was his hope that he might ever speak to Corinne of his love for her. Were he Count of Brives, then would it be a very different thing; for he could hurry back from the war and make haste to deal with those estates which Count Charles treated so ill. But he told himself again and again that all his visions of the night had been phantoms of sleep come to torment him with illusions and vain words. He was still Eugène, the dragoon — with scarce ten gold pieces in his pocket and no prospect for the future save that which the war offered to him. Little Corinne remained the mistress of the Hôtel Beautreillis and of the great station which her possessions gave to her. What folly

THE PURPLE GLASS

to dream that he might ever tell her that he loved her!

Saying this to himself, he made a hurried meal; and all being ready, set out for the Barrière du Trône when the clocks of Paris were striking half-past six. His baggage had gone already in the waggons of the regiment, which he was to join at Chalons; and he rode now accompanied only by his servant Barnardin, who led his second charger. Many turned in the streets to look at the handsome dragoon in the sky-blue uniform; many muttered, "There goes that rogue Sabatier to the wars;" but Eugène noticed none of them. A deep depression weighed him down; his accustomed gaiety and readiness of speech had forsaken him; he struck again into the heart of the woods of Vincennes, and the silence of the thickets was like balm to his weary mind. He was absolutely convinced that the events of the dreadful night were the events of a dream. He remembered that he must pass his brother's château on his way to Chalons. "I will call and ask a God-speed of him," said he to himself; "I owe him that for allowing myself ever to repeat so cruel a calumny."

He had come by this time to that little place upon the hill whence he could look down to the Seine, and observe the gloomy towers of his brother's house. Here, despite his resolution, a shudder of fear trembled upon all his limbs. Strange as he thought it, the dream seemed more real with every mile he rode. He could have sworn that he stood last night upon that very spot; he remembered the blood-red light upon the river; the shiver of the aspens; the foreboding which possessed him. Angry with himself that these thoughts prevailed, he set spurs to his horse, and rode at a gallop toward the village.

"A plague upon it," said he, "it was a dream, a silly dream. I did not sup with my brother, and never shall I be Count of Brives — fool that I am to think of it!"

"Monsieur," said a voice at his side, "permit me to tell you that you are mistaken."

Eugène checked his horse and looked round quickly. He saw to his astonishment that a man who wore a rich dress of black cloth, and a black plumed hat, rode at his side upon a magnificent beast who kept pace with the other as easily as though he had been walking for the show of it in the Place Louis Quinze.

"Monsieur," said the dragoon, civilly, "you said — ?"

"That you are very much mistaken, sir, — you did sup with your brother last night, and you will be Count of Brives before the clock strikes again."

THE PURPLE GLASS

The words were spoken with such a fine air that Sabatier began to ask himself if this were some new apparition come to cheat him as the others had done.

"Oh," cried he, impatiently, "what mystery is all this! Am I in my senses, or do I still sleep?"

He reined in his horse, and the stranger came close up to his side.

"Monsieur," said he, "you neither sleep nor dream. Ask yourself no such silly question. It is quite true that your brother attempted to poison you last night with a flask of Armagnac in which, as the physician Antonio would tell you, there were four grains of one of the most deadly drugs known to the East. You, however, remembering the warning, drank but a half of the glass set before you — and so you become Count of Brives."

"I?" cried Eugene, impatiently, "I become Count of Brives?"

"Exactly," said the other; "you have only to ride to yonder château to make it your own."

The dragoon laughed scornfully.

"Pah!" said he, "how could the wine have been poisoned when my brother drank of it; and how could your physician know what the flask contained?"

The man in the plumed hat betrayed no sign of impatience.

"Monsieur," said he, slowly, "you ask me two questions, and I will answer them. We knew what the wine contained because Armand, your brother's servant, has long been good enough to sell us for money an account of your brother's life. Three weeks ago the Count of Brives was offered by an agent of my mistress, Mademoiselle Corinne, a preparation of the poppy leaf brought from Yezd. So fatal is this to those whose bodies are not fortified against it by the continued and gradual habit of eating the drug, that two-thirds of a grain will kill the strongest man. You, however, drinking but a half of that which was offered to you, suffered but a passing loss of your senses. It is obvious to you that the count, having been long in the East and accustomed to the use of opium, could drink that which would mean the death of another not so prepared. The draught last night steeled his will to the dreadful crime he sought to commit. You, however, succumbed to it; and never, I swear, did the living wear the cloak of the dead as you wore it in the Château Saint Mandé."

Sabatier groaned at the remembrance. It seemed to him that he began to suffer the terror of the garden for the second time.

"*Ciel!*" cried he, "it is all a miracle — I cannot believe it — I cannot."

"It is no miracle," said the stranger, solemnly;

"it is the hand of Almighty God avenging your brother who was slain. Go then to the château — but go alone, that the eyes of no other may witness the deed which must be. I wait here until yonder church bell shall tell me that you are Count of Brives."

He pointed with outstretched arm to the gate of the darkening house upon whose blackened walls the last crimson rays of the setting sun were dying down quickly. As Eugène rode away, he remembered that he had seen the stranger before, and he said — it was he who called from the window last night — " Monsieur le Comte, Monsieur le Comte, where is your brother Eugène?" Drawn on at the recollection as by a fatality, eager to prove, to make sure, now buoyed up with hope, now trembling with excitement, he galloped through the street of the village, and never drew rein until his hand was upon the bell at the outer gate of the château and the birds were winging upward at his clamorous peal. As it had been last night — that night of nights — so was it to-day. The toothless old Armand gave him welcome; the lad Germain held his horse. Nothing seemed altered in the great house; nothing of its silence nor of its mystery. But Sabatier's heart beat until his whole body shook with the pulsations; and so great was his dread that he could scarce frame the question —

"Where is my brother, the count?"

"Monsieur," said the old man, with a horrible leer, "your brother awaits you in the garden."

Bidding him stay where he was, Sabatier ascended the rotting staircase and passed rapidly through the hall. "I will know the truth, I will learn all," he said to himself — determined now that the mystery should blind him no more. Many as were his sensations while he strode across the great dining-room to the garden beyond, he quitted them all in the greater doubt — "Can this thing have been?" And doubting of it to the last, he opened the window and so beheld his brother.

The count was dressed as he had been on the previous evening; but his eyes were now bloodshot and inflamed; his step halting and restless; his hair dishevelled. When Sabatier saw him thus, he was walking, with bent head, to and fro upon the grass plot by the bushes; but his glance was ever upon the ground, and he muttered unceasingly, "Where is my brother Eugène?" This haunting cry had been upon his lips through every hour of that dreadful night. He had never left the scene of his crime — had touched no food, had spoken no word. From the moment when he discovered that some unseen eye watched him in his horrid task — the Count of Brives lost his reason.

"Oh, my God!" cried Eugène, aloud, moved to exceeding pity by a sight so woeful, "my brother is mad."

The count heard the cry and looked up. For one long-drawn instant he stood quite still; then, with a moan upon his lips, he began to walk backwards down the garden. But at the third step, he fell heavily upon the grass.

"Brother," said Eugène, running to his side, — "brother, I forgive."

It was a word of surpassing love — but the heart of the Count of Brives had ceased to beat when it was spoken.

When Eugène Sabatier rode from the Château Saint Mandé that night to join the army at Chalons, the villagers cried after him, —

"*Bon soir*, Monsieur le Comte."

And the bells of the little church soon told all Paris that Charles, Count of Brives, was no more.

THE KINGDOM OF BOURGORIEAU

VI

THE KINGDOM OF BOURGORIEAU

THE Feast of the Precious Blood, on the fourth day of July, in the year 1763, sent many of Old Paris to the gardens of the *Courtille des Porcherons*, famous at that time for the great sign-board upon which Master Ramponeau, the host of the *guinguette*, was depicted, sitting astride a hogshead, and therefrom beckoning all the city to taste of his unsurpassable wines. Other *courtilles*, it is true, waged a good fight against the booths and bazaars of the *Tambour Royal*, as old Ramponeau's house was called; but the fame of his tavern was built upon the rock of a royal patronage, and rare was the day when some masquerader from the palace did not drive to that place of arbours and of shade in quest of adventure which should oil his tongue at Trianon. Thither, too, went the butter girls from the Quai de Gesvres, ready with their pretty patois to answer the dragoons of the guard — thither, as rumour said, Madame herself had gone under the escort of the Duc de Richelieu. Bourgeois or aristocrat, priest or clerk, student or philosopher, trooper or captain, — it mattered not in the gardens of Ramponeau. He had the same welcome for all — the same witty greeting, the same civility. And he knew more of the secrets of Paris than the Canons of Notre Dame themselves. "Oh, ce bon Ramponeau, comme il est drôle," said the women. The men spoke of his wines. There were no better in Paris. To drink them you could suffer even the music of Ramponeau's fiddler and the dust of the drive to the Porcherons.

The Feast of the Precious Blood was a day of sun and heat; but a cool breeze came up with the evening, and many masqueraders gathered at the hour of eight o'clock in the shady avenues of the *Tambour Royal*. Ramponeau, whose long neck twisted unrestingly in his greetings to this great man or to that, was hoarse with proclaiming the merits of his wine of Burgundy and of his Armagnac. The weary fiddler in the great tent beat his instrument savagely, as though angry with it and the world which compelled him. The jaded dancers had abandoned the more stately steps of the Basque for the fever of the Poitou jig. Everywhere in the cool of the gardens the lovers walked — here a wit of Trianon impatient at the slow understanding of a Corydon; there a dragoon, who told himself that the masked unknown who clung

THE KINGDOM OF BOURGORIEAU

timorously to his arm must certainly be a duchess. Uniforms, gorgeous in gold and lace, were to be observed through a tracery of boughs and leaves still green — the scarlet of the gendarmerie, the blue of the Corsican legion, the towering brass helmets of Condé's men. Even cassocked priests took pleasure with circumspection, and drank the wines of Italy served from dainty flasks. So great was the press of aristocrat and of citizen that a table apart was a possession of great price. One man alone in all the throng commanded such a privilege and was not denied. He was Bourgorieau, the king's swordsman.

A man of small stature, slightly pock-marked yet pleasant of countenance, with a beard trimmed in the Spanish fashion, and a suit of violet cloth to cover a frame of iron, — such was Bourgorieau, the swordsman. Many turned to look at him when they passed, but none so long as to draw upon himself the gaze of one who was the master even of the masters of his art. At any other time, perhaps, in the garden of the Tuileries or the theatre of the palace, it had been possible to exchange a greeting with this man of Nantes, whose sword had cut for him such a broad road to fame. But at the *Tambour Royal*, such a thing was not to be thought of. Even Ramponeau would cease to twist his long neck, and to speak of Armagnac when he approached the arbour of wild roses before the doors of which the *maître d'armes* sat. Swaggering troopers ceased to swagger when they beheld the pock-marked face and the suit of violet. Even a dancing girl had not the temerity to thrust out her tambourine for the sous of Bourgorieau. He sat alone, silent, asking friendship of none nor seeking it.

It was seven o'clock when Bourgorieau entered the tavern of old Ramponeau; it was half past eight before he remembered that Javotte, his daughter, would be waiting for him in the little house upon the island of St. Louis. She would have supper prepared against his coming. He was not one who cared very much for the hospitality of taverns; nor would he have gone to the *Tambour Royal* at all had not the vanity of his art compelled him. While men said that he was a sullen rogue who sat apart because of the grim shadows upon his life, he, in turn, was telling himself that it was good to observe the fear of his fellows and to assert, wherever it might be, that title of mastership which his sword had won for him so readily in Paris. For the poltroons who passed swiftly by his table he felt nothing but contempt; but the contempt was a thought of gain; and he reminded himself often that it would be a bad day for him when men ceased to remark his coming or to give him the

THE KINGDOM OF BOURGORIEAU

chief seats in the *guinguette*. For the rest, the tipsy masquerader, the hollow wit, the glitter of colour and the music of fiddlers, he cared not at all. His life lay in his house, in the love of child and home. His arm had quivered many a time when he stood to the encounter and told himself that he might never see Javotte again. Yet the world said he did not know fear. He laughed at the world and kept his secret.

The tavern clock chimed the hour; the throng was increasing in the grove when the king's swordsman drained his glass of Chianti and began to feel in his pocket for a crown wherewith to pay the score of old Ramponeau. He was upon the point of rising from the table when an exclamation uttered by one who passed by caused him to look up quickly and to discover that he was no longer alone in the arbour. A young man, shabbily dressed in a suit of brown cloth and carrying a traveller's bundle upon his shoulder, had left the ranks of the masqueraders to trespass upon that forbidden ground which all Paris had conceded to the Kingdom of Bourgorieau. So quick had the action been, so little expected, that none put out a hand to touch the youth upon the shoulder or to tell him whither he went. Seeming to know nothing of the place or the people, the stranger advanced boldly to the sacred table, upon which he cast his bundle with the air of one very much fatigued. Then he fell rather than sat in the chair which awaited any person fortunate enough to enjoy the hospitality of the *maître d'armes*. The half-suppressed exclamation of anger which the swordsman uttered was lost upon him. He saw nothing of the gaping amazement of those who stood in the shadow of the trees; he did not hear the words of sympathy and surprise which the women uttered.

"*Oh, c'est ben,*" he exclaimed, as he sat, and his idiom was that of Eastern France. "I have walked far, monsieur, and there is dust upon the road to Strasbourg. You will let me sit a little while at your table and drink a cup of wine with you?"

Bourgorieau looked upon the lad as upon some curiosity fallen from the heavens at his feet. His first thought had been to call for a cudgel and to thrash the impertinent fellow soundly; but the music of the young man's voice, his soft, pleasing, almost girlish face, his tremendous ignorance, stayed the other's hand. He glanced quickly to that place between the trees where the carousal was at its height, and saw that many waited for him to act. How if he did not humour them? he asked himself. It was a pleasing whim, this idea of suffering the stranger at his table. And if any came to question him he would know how to answer.

"So you are from Strasbourg, *mon vieux*," he said, surprised not a little at the sound of his own voice, "and yet you come in by the Porte St. Denis?"

"I live by the lodge of Neuilly," answered the youth, simply; "to-morrow, if all goes well, I shall see my home again — but first I have my work to do in Paris, and it is for that I am come to this tavern. Oh, surely, sir, these are very great people, and I shall hear from them of him whom I seek. Is not this the house of Maître Ramponeau, whom even the queen has honoured? They said so out yonder. 'You will find him,' they said, and I know they speak well. To-morrow I shall go on again — the work will be done, it must be done, for God has willed it."

He laid his head upon his arms wearily, as though all the light and music of the house could not keep sleep from his eyes. Bourgorieau knew not what chord of sympathy was struck at the note of the young man's voice, but somehow he began to think of Javotte waiting for him at home. He said that they would make a pretty pair — this curly headed lad of Strasbourg who talked so blithely of having work to do and the little maid of his own house who alone in all Paris could find love for him. He was half a mind to bid the stranger follow him to the island of St. Louis and there to share his supper; but first he asked a question, and the answer to it was a word to set him laughing as he had not laughed since he left the *salle d'armes* of old Andrea at Nantes.

"You say, lad, that you are looking for some one in Paris? Who is he that his business should bring him to this tavern?"

"I seek Bourgorieau, he whom they call the king's swordsman. You know him, monsieur?"

Bourgorieau leaned back in his chair and stared, open-mouthed, at the speaker.

"If I know him — what then?"

"Be so good as to tell me where I may find the man who murdered my father."

Bourgorieau laughed so loudly that many came out of the grove to listen. "It is his son who has returned," said some; others, that he had drunk overmuch Burgundy. But the stranger neither laughed with the *maître d'armes* nor observed those who watched him so curiously.

"I am Lucien," he continued, "the son of Georges Duroc, who was killed in this tavern eight years ago, monsieur. I was a boy then, but to-day I am a man. I come to Paris to do the work appointed to me. Laugh as you please, I know well that God sends me here, and that my journey will not be in vain. To-morrow Bourgorieau will be dead and I shall be in my mother's house again."

THE KINGDOM OF BOURGORIEAU

He spoke neither loudly nor with a boaster's voice. In his eyes there was a light as of a spiritual force working in his mind and creating visions for him. Bourgorieau laughed no longer. The frail and prettily rounded arms, the white skin, the gentle face of the youth were forgotten by him. He recalled, rather, the day when he had killed Georges Duroc in that very garden. Some trivial excuse of insult had served for the deed of that night. And this was the man's son — sent, as he said, by God to demand a reckoning. Bourgorieau tried to laugh scornfully at all superstitions. He told himself that he could fight this lad of Strasbourg with a bandage over his eyes. But his mouth was parched when he sought to answer the youth; and he called to one near him to send another flask of Chianti.

"So you are Lucien Duroc," he said, when he had drunk a deep draught, "and you come here to settle with old Bourgorieau? *Ma foi!* you have a fine conceit, my friend."

Lucien sipped at the wine offered to him and began to bind his bundle more securely.

"Monsieur," he replied very earnestly, "you do not understand me; I do not know if I understand these things myself, for they are God's mysteries. It is true, as you say, that Maître Bourgorieau is the first blade in Paris; we have heard even in

Strasbourg of the things he has done and the favour he has won. For myself, I have not held a sword in my hand but two or three times in all my life. How then, you ask, shall I bring such a one to his account? Sir, I know not what answer I can make if it be not to tell you of all the things I have heard and seen in the long nights of this last year at Strasbourg. Oh, monsieur, the gate of heaven has been opened for me, and I have heard the Divine voice commanding me that I should arise and go to Paris and do this thing. Often in my dreams have I heard the voices bidding me to leave the city and to delay no longer. 'Seek and you shall find, and the angels shall keep watch over you,' they said always. Sir, should I fear any man because I have listened to the message and have come here as I am commanded? Am I not right to say that to-morrow the justice of Heaven will fall upon him who killed my father, and that I shall go back to my mother's house and tell her to mourn no more for him whom we loved, but to be glad because justice has been done? I am young, and I know that my life is before me. I have seen gardens of flowers in my sleep, and have walked there with those who will be with me to my life's end. I have stood upon the banks of a great river, and the sweet breezes have blown upon my face, and I have heard the message that I shall

THE KINGDOM OF BOURGORIEAU

follow the river to the new country of my dreams. Life is sweet to me, for I am young; but I shall not lose my life because God sends me to Paris; there is none that can harm me while I go to my duty and defend my father's honour. Think not, monsieur, that I boast when I say that to-morrow Bourgorieau will be dead. The king himself could not save him now; it is written in the book of fate, and no human hand shall blot that writing out."

He rose from the table at the words and took up his bundle as though the rest were in itself the enemy of his mission. Bourgorieau, who had sat white and silent while he spoke, now awoke as from a spell and touched the speaker upon the arm.

"Sit," he said in a low voice, — "sit and tell me more of these dreams of yours, my friend. Who knows that this meeting is not written also in the book you name!"

Lucien rested his bundle upon the table. Bourgorieau saw that his hands trembled; there was in his eyes the light of the mystic awakened, of the dreamer made strong by the fevers of dreams.

"What will it serve me to tell you if you cannot bring me face to face with the man I seek?" he asked.

"Has he no love of life too?" asked Bourgorieau, upon whose forehead heavy drops of sweat were starting. "Has he no home to which he would return; is there none there to welcome his coming or to mourn if he should not go back? Would you make me the servant of his murderer, Monsieur Lucien? Nay, how shall I answer to his child — how shall I tell her — ?"

"You shall say that you are the servant of a servant of God, monsieur. Yet do not think that I compel you if your will is not in this matter. The same hand which beckoned me from Strasbourg will point the way still. I seek the aid of none — the friendship of none. I need no courage nor skill. To-morrow my work will be done, for the voices have promised so — to-morrow Paris will know of it. And the world will be a better world for the death of this man, monsieur."

He bowed with the grace of one born to high place, and before the other could arrest him, disappeared in the grove. For many minutes after he had gone, Bourgorieau sat staring at the masqueraders as though some after-thought would send the youth back to him and permit that opportunity of defence and argument of which surprise had robbed him. But the throng passed on, the music of the fiddlers waxed more discordant, the laughter was shriller and more brutal; and still the old swordsman sat alone. There were moments, in truth,

THE KINGDOM OF BOURGORIEAU

when he believed that he had dreamed of the youth's coming and of the words he remembered so distinctly. But this did not help him to shake off the strange foreboding which now began to possess him. It seemed to him that some miracle must have sent the lad to the gardens of the *Tambour Royal.* He recalled the boyish face, the dreamy eyes, the spiritual enthusiasm of Lucien's quest. He remembered his confession, that he knew nothing of the sword, and fell to uttering the names of those great fencers who had fallen in a brawl with the untutored or the unskilled. Minute by minute his fear magnified. How if this were, indeed, the justice of God come to overtake him, he asked himself. None had dared to tell him hitherto that Paris would be a better city for his death. The words which Lucien had uttered so solemnly echoed in his ears — "it is written in the book." All the superstitions of the superstitious West crowded upon his mind. He laughed aloud to think of them, yet racked his brain the more for any omen of the past which would explain away the mystery of the night. When he left the garden at last, he staggered through the press blindly, caring nothing for the muttered curses which followed him. At the gate of the tavern he told himself that he was already a rich man, and had promised himself some day a home in Nantes among his own people and the children of his boyhood.

The great clock of Notre Dame was striking eleven when Bourgorieau crossed the moonlit Pont Mairie and beheld again the lamp set in the latticed window of his house upon the island. Crooked and gabled and lofty, the neighbour of the little church of Saint Louis of the Isle, leaning against other houses which had looked down upon the Paris of the dark ages, the tumbling building, nevertheless, was to him a palace of palaces. Here he could forget the intrigue of court and camp; the slights of those before whom he must cringe; the slanders of his unnumbered enemies. Here all pomp and ceremony were forgotten; here, it was not his to serve nor to remember the darker side of service. At this hour of night, the city around him was hushed in the silence of sleep. So clear was the sky that the stars seemed to have come down very near to the earth, and to hang like golden lamps in the grey vault of the night. The swirling river lapped rhythmically upon the piles of the old bridge. By here and there, a belated citizen clattered across the flags and went tipsily to his home. The guard paced his beat with measured and echoing steps.

Bourgorieau stood for a long while watching the light in his house. He could see Javotte as

"It is thou, Dear Father."

THE KINGDOM OF BOURGORIEAU

she waited at the window; a childish figure, weary with the vigil. He knew that the sound of his steps would animate that figure presently, would bring laughter to the sleepy eyes. He pictured the moment when he would hold her in his arms and read the joy of love written upon her face; the face of the one being in Paris who was sad at his going; who counted the hours that should bring him back again. And watching her, he heard, as though a voice answered from the shadows, the words of Lucien Duroc in the gardens of Ramponeau, "Arise and go." Even as the voices had spoken to the lad, so now they warned him. "To-morrow," he said, "it would be too late. Javotte would wait at the window as of old time, but the vigil would be eternal. Never again would the joy of her love shine in the eyes of the child; never again—"

Bourgorieau hurried on. The guard standing in the shadow of the church heard a child's voice, sweet and melodious, above the murmur of the river,—

"It is thou, dear father; oh, how long I have watched for thee, how long—"

. . . .

At ten o'clock upon the following morning, a horseman rode at a gallop into the great courtyard of Versailles. To the many who asked him what news, he answered only, "He is gone; the wager is won." But to the Duc de Richelieu who waited for him in the gardens of Trianon he told a better story.

"All Paris talks of nothing else," he said. "The king must hear of it at once. Last night at the house of Ramponeau, Mademoiselle Corinne of the Hôtel Beautreillis wagered that she would drive Bourgorieau, the bully, from the city before twenty hours had passed. She dressed as a lad of Strasbourg and prated of a divine mission. This morning, the man set out for Nantes, taking his daughter with him. He will come here no more, Monsieur le Duc — Saint John, that I should be the first with such news —"

The duke stopped in his walk and gazed openmouthed at the messenger.

"How — Bourgorieau is gone — you say he will not come back —"

"I say well, or if he come it will be his last visit. Paris knows now that he is a coward, and twenty blades will be ready for him. We live in a day of miracles, and this is one of them. But I go to the king lest others be before me. A thousand crowns — *ma foi*, she should have won ten thousand!"

. . . .

Bourgorieau heard of the jest in his home at

THE KINGDOM OF BOURGORIEAU

Nantes. He answered those who told him by showing them the house he had built and the garden he had planted. They heard Javotte singing there, yet wondered at his indifference.

"I care not," he said, "for she who was sent came to me from God."

THE DEVIL'S BOWL AND THE STRANGE AFFAIR AT FONTENAY

VII

THE DEVIL'S BOWL AND THE STRANGE AFFAIR AT FONTENAY

CORINNE DE MONTESSON leant back in her coach and sighed. Paris seemed so far off; the woods of Fontenay were so dark and gloomy that she began to think the sun would never shine for her again.

"Antonio," she said, speaking to the old physician who sat opposite to her, and asking him a question which she had asked ten times since they were driven through the deserted street of Noisy le Grand — "Antonio, what time is it?"

Antonio, who was making what use he could of the passing daylight to complete a calculation which engrossed him, put down his book and began to observe the surrounding woods very closely.

"Mademoiselle," said he presently, "it is the hour of sunset on the third day of April in the year 1764."

Corinne laughed when she heard this very precise statement, and nestling her ruddy cheeks against the cushion of the coach, she fell to watching Antonio, who dipped his pen regularly into an ink-horn slung at his waist, and held his book close to the window that the last rays of the sinking sun might fall upon it. When she had watched him a little while, and, after that, had counted the trees which flashed by as the coach rolled down the hill of Fontenay until she had numbered three hundred, she spoke again, —

"Antonio, you know where we are?"

The old physician stopped in the middle of shaping an 8 and put his head out of the window.

"Mademoiselle," he said, "we are half of a league from the town of Fontenay at the spot known as the Gorge of the Three Gibbets, reminding us that very lately his Majesty has caused three rogues to be hanged in this place."

Corinne laughed again.

"My dear Antonio," she said, "what a guide you would make!"

Antonio picked up his pen.

"My child," said he, "unless we observe the signposts as we go, life is likely to show us a heavy road. For my part, I forget nothing when I am assured that it is worth remembering."

"You would say that of Fontenay, Antonio?"

"Certainly, mademoiselle, I would say that of Fontenay. Strange indeed, if I forgot the place where they robbed and killed my poor friend the Count of Charny."

Corinne shuddered. She remembered that dreadful story well. The darkening woods around her, the silence of the gloomy plantations, the phantomlike shape of tree and bush, compelled her to realise very forcibly in what a dangerous place she was, and how pleased she would be to see the lights of Paris again.

"Oh," she said, "you are a poor comforter, Antonio — to speak of that affair now, when Bénoît remains at Gros Bois and we ride alone."

Antonio closed his book with a snap, for the light no longer permitted him to read.

"Mademoiselle," he said, "do you say that you ride alone when I am with you?"

"Not at all, my dear Antonio; I said that *we* ride alone — and lack any protector save the good will which some of these men bear to me. What a poor thing is that to rely upon! I am sure that I was very foolish to leave Bénoît behind. The sword is with thieves a better weapon than a thief's charity, *mon ami*. And was there ever such a swordsman as Bénoît?"

Antonio shrugged his shoulders.

"All that you claim for our kinsman, that I will admit," said he; "yet when you would praise the sword as a weapon, mademoiselle, then you speak as one who knows nothing of the greater mysteries. I, who am a child with the rapier in my hand, can become the equal of thousands of armies when I turn to those allies which exist neither in matter nor in the schools — but here, in thought, in conception, in, if you will, my dreams.

"To-night you ask for your kinsman and his strong arm, yet, believe me, my daughter, should misfortune overtake us, I, who have no weapon but my book, no ally but my visions, will prove the better friend. Not that I anticipate any such necessity. Another hour will see us at the barrier; we shall pass Fontenay itself before the clock strikes again. Take courage, then, mademoiselle, and forget that the sun no longer shines, and that night is in the woods."

Corinne, who never ceased to enjoy the pompous self-assurance and the egotistical pronouncements of old Antonio, laughed in her sleeve now, and, having laughed, she buried her head in the cushions, and suffered stoically the terrible lurchings and rollings of the rut-tossed coach. After all, she said, her name was a great name amongst the robbers about Paris, and he would be a daring fellow who would venture to stop her carriage. She recalled again how she had won a pardon for the notorious Coq le Roi, who had narrated the deed in a hundred taverns since then, and had made of her, all unwillingly, a very *déesse* among patrons.

Should any one now attack her, she thought that it would be sufficient if her lacqueys mentioned her name. Nor did she rely at all upon the mysterious boasts and promises of the old physician, who had forgotten them already, and slept soundly with his half-open book lying neglected at his feet.

The coach rolled on deeper and deeper into the hollow of the night. By here and there the trees were so thick that the lantern which a lacquey had kindled scarce saved them from the ditch. At other times you could see a little way into the clearings of the thickets, or espy dark and noxious pools suggesting solitude and terrible deeds and the gloomy mystery of woodland life.

Corinne needed all her courage to banish the thoughts suggested by the scenes, but she had a mind powerful in obedience, and when her first alarms had passed, she compelled herself to think of the gaiety and life of Paris, and of all she would do during her long summer there. Indeed, she had made some very pretty plans for herself, and was in fancy dancing a minuet with the king, when a loud report of a musket, followed by a great clamour of question and answer and the sudden stopping of the coach, awoke her from her dream ; and all her little castles came tumbling on the ground.

QUEEN OF THE JESTERS

"Antonio, Antonio!" she cried, "do you not [see that] they have stopped the coach, Antonio [make] haste to tell them who I am. Oh, if I [had] left Bénoît at Gros Bois!"

Antonio, who woke with a start, stopped a mo-[ment to] pick up his book; then he put his head [out of the] window, but drew it back upon the [instant.]

"Mademoiselle," said he, "there are three men, [and they] are tying your lacqueys to the trees."

[Corinne,] ashamed of her first alarms, attempted [to laugh, but] the laugh had a quaver of fear in it.

"My dear Antonio," she exclaimed, "pray [make] haste to tell the gentlemen whose coach [this is.]"

Antonio, thus commanded, put his head out of [the] window for the second time, and began to [address the] robbers.

"Sirs," said he, "I beg a word with you. This [coach] of Mademoiselle Corinne de Montes-[pan, whose] name, I make sure, is very well known [to you."]

To the physician's surprise the three men made [him no ans]wer at all, but continued quietly to bind [the hand]s of the lacqueys and then to tie them to [the neares]t trees. When they had done their work, the tallest of the three, who was dressed in black and silver and wore a mask upon his face, came up to the door of the coach and opened it. At the same time he doffed his cap and bowed with the dignity of a courtier.

"Mademoiselle," said he, addressing Corinne, "a thousand pardons for the liberty we have taken. Be assured that I know your name well and that it is held in great reverence here. But·I have laid a wager of a thousand crowns that you shall sup with me to-night at the house of the Silver Birch, and that I shall kiss you on both cheeks afterwards. Accord me, I beg of you, a favour so trifling, and earn the lasting gratitude of Claude Brissac."

He stood up, a fine figure even in the sombre flare of the two torches which his companions had kindled, and now held aloft that Corinne might see to alight. Very bright eyes shone humorously beneath the velvet mask; diamonds sparkled upon the ample ruffles of lace at his wrist and throat.

Corinne had heard his name often. It was that of one of the most gallant and successful highwaymen upon the eastern roads to Paris. "La Force" they called him, for his unquenchable energy and his unfailing boldness. Corinne knew that such a man would allow nothing to turn him from his purpose, and she trembled a little when she answered him.

"Monsieur," she said in her own pretty way, "I cannot think that you would compel me against my will. I would eat of your supper very gladly, did you choose other opportunity to invite me. But I must be in Paris to-night, and I rely upon you to hasten my journey thither. Indeed, I am sure that you will do so."

"Saint Denis!" replied the man, "and gladly would I help you. Yet, mademoiselle, if you will but reflect a little, you will see how reasonable is my request. It must be plain to you, since your lacqueys are now keeping company with yonder trees, while your coachman is shedding tears in the ditch, that you cannot arrive in Paris before dawn at any rate. What more pleasant occupation, then, than a little supper — where, be assured, the homage due to so great a name shall be fully paid. Let this old man hasten to get out of the coach, that I may have the pleasure of feeling your pretty hand upon my arm."

He held his plumed hat still in his hand, and his manner was in all things the manner of Trianon. Corinne did not fail to see that no words of hers would turn him from his purpose; but old Antonio was by no means so willing to surrender readily.

"Sir," cried he, "you are a very impertinent fellow; if you do not have a care, all Paris will come presently to see you hang at your own door."

"Saint John!" said the robber, grimly, "if that day come, old man, surely I will ask for the halter which thou hast worn. Get down, lest I hasten thy steps with my boot."

Then, turning to Corinne, he continued: —

"Mademoiselle, our supper is getting cold while we wait. Bid this old man be silent, I implore you, lest injury befall him. You have heard of me, I doubt not, and will know how little I am disposed to take 'no' for my answer when I have set my mind upon a 'yes.' 'La Force,' they call me, mademoiselle, as I shall call you my friend presently."

He bowed again, and seeing that Antonio still hesitated, he put his hand roughly upon the physician's collar and dragged him from the coach. Corinne, on her part, convinced that further resistance was useless, stepped lightly from the carriage and took the robber's arm.

"Monsieur," she said, "I am trusting to you as to one of my own kinsmen. But I warn you that you will find me a dangerous guest."

The robber laughed.

"Mademoiselle," said he, "my own daughter shall not win greater respect. You have but to command and I obey."

"In that case," said she, "I beg you permit my lacqueys to accompany me, and to bring the coach to your house, so that when we have supped I can continue my journey."

He answered her very gallantly, —

"Your lacqueys are even now following us — and look, your coachman is again upon his box. If they no longer carry pistols, mademoiselle, it is that they may not shoot themselves. Take my word for it, they will never shoot any one else."

He laughed gaily, and gave the pretty white arm which rested upon his own the suspicion of a squeeze. Had Corinne been certain that the adventure would have begun and ended with the supper at the house of the Silver Birch, her alarm would have been less. As it was, she had a great dread of her company and of the very dark wood which the highwayman now entered.

As for old Antonio, he stumbled along behind her, muttering to himself like a man demented. But he still carried his book, his pen, and his inkhorn; and now and then, had there been light whereby to observe it, a meaning smile might have been seen playing upon his usually placid face. The lacqueys, on the other hand, were in the last stages of fear; and while the coachman cried out that his coach would surely be found in the ditch, the others behind clung to their straps desperately and rolled against each other as men drunk with wine. It was five minutes before this strange cavalcade reached the house of the Silver Birch.

The robber's house lay snug in the thicket as a nest in the hedge. Save for a small clearing near the door, where a stagnant pool gleamed as with the face of a blackened mirror, the copse put walls of bramble and of bracken about the simple chalet, and so sheltered it that only the eyes of a woodlander might detect a habitation in the vicinity.

Nor did there seem to be any one to guard a retreat so remarkable. Not a light shone from the windows when the guests arrived; not a dog barked or a sound made itself heard. Corinne, who was shivering with the rasping air of the night and the noxious and humid miasma of the swamp, began at last to be seriously alarmed. Her coach, perforce, had been left in the more open glade a hundred yards from the robber's home.

"La Force" was accompanied now by one only of the torch-bearers. He had left the other heavily armed to watch the terrified lacqueys. Old Antonio in his turn had become green with anger and cold and impatience. He mumbled no longer, even to himself. The highwayman alone remained self-possessed and talkative; indeed, he assumed a more plausible politeness with every step he took.

"Mademoiselle," he said, producing a great key

from his pocket, and bidding his fellow hold the flambeau nearer to the door, "why do you tremble? Am I not here to protect you? In half an hour you shall have eaten a good supper, and be on your way to Paris again. Judge me not harshly since my honour is at stake."

Corinne stamped her foot.

"Your honour, monsieur!" she cried; "if that be at stake, then surely the wager is trifling."

"Saint John! madame, it is no trifle, since my honour intrusts to me so precious a charge."

He spoke with exceeding deference, and stood bareheaded, despite the raw cold of the night, while he threw open the door for her to enter, and bade the torch-bearer hold up the light. None the less did Corinne continue to tremble when she passed into the house and found herself at once in the chief room of it. She asked only that the adventure might draw quickly to its end, for she felt very helpless, and thought how different it would have been had Bénoit accompanied her from Gros Bois. As for her old physician, who had been so ready with his boasts and his talk of mysteries, she could have laughed aloud at his undisguised distress. The shadow of death seemed already upon him. He started at every sound.

The robber entered the house, and, quickly divesting himself of his heavy cloak and his mask, he lighted candles in a heavy silver candelabrum. Directly the pale yellow light flooded the room, Corinne uttered a little word of surprise, for she had never thought that so poor a house could afford such a feast to the eye as this room now presented. Though the chalet itself was rough hewn of wood from the surrounding thickets, its internal ornament was worthy of the Louvre. Rare tapestries hid bare walls; dainty cabinets filled with fine china, chairs and tables reflecting the delicate taste of the period, a fine copy of the Apollo and Marsyas of Raphael, a genuine sketch by Jean de Paris, another by Rigaud, added to the wealth of its decoration.

Corinne felt her feet sinking into soft white skins the moment she passed the door of the house. A blazing fire of fagots spangled with golden stars the polished wood of the ingle-nook. The table itself was almost hidden by bouquets of spring flowers and early fruits. The whole place was redolent with the air of dishes steaming, and of good things made ready.

"Come," said "La Force," when he had indicated the seat of honour, and had placed Corinne therein, "you will forgive me that I have no lacqueys as you have, mademoiselle. I am a lover of solitude, and my secrets are not well worn in company. But you will find my supper none the less excellent, believe me. As for our friend here, let there be no hot blood between us. I have not forgotten the service he did to Coq le Roi. Saint John! it is I who should fear with such a wizard for my guest."

The bloodless eyes of the old physician twinkled when the compliment was paid. He, for the first time, appeared to forget the pass to which things had come, and to observe the supper now being served by the comrade of their host. When at length he sat down, a smile of satisfaction played upon his face, and he hastened to admit so much to the robber.

"Monsieur," said he, "it is to my mistress that your friend Coq le Roi owes thanks. My own share in that business is not worthy of mention."

"*Ciel!*" cried the robber, helping Corinne to a goblet of Chianti, "you are modest, Monsieur le Médecin; did you not, as the story goes, tell the lieutenant of police everything that Coq le Roi was about to do during the next four-and-twenty hours? Holy Mother of God! I would have given a hundred crowns had I been there to hear the jest."

Antonio looked up from his plate.

"My friend," said he, "it was a jest, I grant; yet had it been my intention, I could have told the future of Coq le Roi not for one day, but for a year."

" La Force" roared with laughter; the wine had warmed him, and his wager was nearly won.

" Name of the devil," cried he, " you are a true magician, old man; have a care lest you provoke me to ask a like experiment."

" Indeed," intervened Corinne, who had exchanged a quick glance with the doctor, " you do Antonio an injustice. A very little provocation, Monsieur Brissac, will induce him to grant your request. He has been absorbed in some calculation ever since we left Gros Bois."

" La Force" drained a goblet to the dregs.

"Saint Denis!" said he, " we will put him to the proof upon the spot. Did not Coq le Roi tell me that he drew little lines upon a piece of paper? Very well, then, your physician has paper, mademoiselle, and I see an ink-horn at his waist. Let him tell me what I shall be doing this time tomorrow night. If he can do that, I will conduct you to your coach before the clock strikes again."

Corinne looked at Antonio inquiringly, but the doctor shook his head.

" It is true," said he, " that I told Coq le Roi's fate, and traced the orbit of his day; but that, I would ask you to remember, was a jest. To-night we leave the jester's mask behind us, and neither pen nor paper will serve our purpose. Command, I pray you, monsieur, that your servant bring me yon silver bowl full to the brim with boiling water."

"Pah!" exclaimed the robber, "you think that I am a child!"

"I think nothing, monsieur. I wait to act. But if you do not choose—"

"La Force" shrugged his shoulders; the wine had quickened his more brutal instincts.

"Oh," replied he, "as for that — I choose; but I tell you plainly, *mon ami*, if this be another of your jests, you shall drain the bowl to the dregs."

Had the robber been sober enough to detect it, he would have observed that old Antonio's eyes were lighted for a moment by a look which boded no good to him. But he was too busy with the flagons of wine, and the excellent supper his fellow rogue had cooked, to observe it, and the look passed upon the instant, to leave the physician unmoved and apparently unconcerned. Even a close observer would not have foretold anything of the comedy then about to be played in the house of the Silver Birch.

None the less, Corinne foretold it. A subtle instinct warned her from the first that her old friend had not forgotten altogether his boasts in the coach. She knew not what plan he had contrived, nor what weapon he sought; but she began to take heart, hoping that she might, after all, be revenged on this insolent fellow who had subjected her to such an insult. In truth, her pride was sore hurt; and although she hid her feelings very prettily, nevertheless she told herself that the highwayman known as "La Force" should find her, as she had declared, a dangerous guest.

All this passed through her mind when the lesser rogue, who aped the rôle of lacquey, brought the silver bowl from the kitchen, and the steam from the boiling water began to moisten the air of the supper-room. Antonio had now tucked up the sleeves of his heavy gown, and was prepared, apparently, to fulfil his promise to the ultimate letter.

"Monsieur Brissac, you have asked me to tell you upon what employment you will be engaged at this hour to-morrow night. When the steam from that bowl shall have cleared away, I will ask you to look at the surface of the water, and to read your own fate therein."

The robber laughed scornfully.

"At your pleasure, friend," said he, "though if you fail me, I warrant you I will keep my word."

Antonio bowed, but said nothing. Corinne felt her heart beating quickly, while the blood surged up into her head and made her dizzy. She began to fear that Antonio was embarked upon some very dangerous enterprise, in which failure might leave her alone with this ruffian who had stopped her coach. She was tempted almost to beg her friend to desist, but he refused steadfastly to exchange a glance with her, and she, by a great effort of will, held her peace.

A minute passed, perhaps, before the steam floated away from the circle of the bowl. When it was quite clear Antonio rose from his chair and began to peer into the water very diligently.

"Monsieur," said he, with great dignity, "come near and tell me if the water of life has any message for you."

The robber bent over the bowl, and examined its contents very narrowly. "Bah!" he answered, "you mock me; there is nothing there."

Antonio looked again.

"My son," said he, speaking now with the air of a doctor, "fate is not the child of man, that he shall say to her, do this, and she will do it. Seek rather to approach these mysteries with awe, for they are mysteries to which God alone holds the key. Let there be obedience in your heart and humility in your mind, since the hour of your death is about to be made known to you."

"Monsieur," said he, "for the third time, I tell you, beware how you jest with me."

In spite of his braggadocio, "La Force" trembled.

STRANGE AFFAIR AT FONTENAY

His hand shook a little when he bent over the table; the colour rushed from his face and his lips were bloodless.

"Speak not of jests, I say," cried the old physician, solemnly, — "speak not of jests, for the book of God is about to be opened before your eyes. Nay, my son, let there be a prayer upon your lips, and the fear of God in your mind. Behold, the picture shapes itself."

Swiftly and deftly he took a phial from his pocket and cast the contents upon the face of the water. The robber, wound up to a surpassing dread and curiosity, bent over the bowl until his eyes almost touched the water. At the same moment the white powder from the phial began to mix with the liquid and to set up a great effervescence, with a noxious odour which filled the whole room: a seething vapour, which hurt the lungs of those who breathed it. "La Force," who all unwillingly inhaled the vapour as he bent over the water, uttered a loud cry and made to draw back from the table; but old Antonio had gripped him by the neck now, and was strong with the strength of ten men.

"Behold, my son, behold, and read the book of life," he cried, with a ferocity which was almost devilish, while he forced the robber's head down until his brow touched the silver rim. "Did I not tell you that the hour of your death was written there? — look well then, for the hour is come."

During a terrible instant, the struggle was a doubtful one. The bowl rocked and spilt the water upon the table; glasses fell and were crunched under the elbows of the men; the robber, about whose throat the bony fingers of the physician were twined, fought like a wild beast. For the first fumes of the drug had robbed him of breath, almost of sense; his lungs were scorched as by burning needles; his eyes were blinded and smarting; it seemed as though a hand of iron had been put upon his heart to still it.

Presently sense began to leave him; and after a moment of suffering, when he thought that he was sinking down, down into a vast abyss of darkness, the idea began to recur in his mind that he was lapping the water of the bowl; and this quickened and quickened, as ideas will in the brains of those who are on the point of losing sensibility, until he sank as one dead upon the floor, and silence fell upon the room again.

Silence fell upon the room, but half of a minute was not marked on the clock before it was broken. The robber's comrade, awakened to curiosity by the hush of voices, appeared suddenly at the door of the supper-room, and stood half choked by the vapours. Corinne herself was upon the point of fainting, when the old physician unbarred the shutters of the little window, and let the night breeze come blowing in like a gift of life.

"Mademoiselle," said he, "stand here at the window, and your faintness will pass; I am going to deal with this fellow as I have dealt with his master."

The second of the robbers gave a great cry, for he saw the body of "La Force" huddled upon the floor, and did not neglect to observe the broken glasses and the disordered table.

"Holy God!" exclaimed he, "'La Force' is dead."

"As you say, my friend," answered Antonio, "'La Force' is dead. Let me conjure you to leave this house quickly, lest my art strike you as it has struck him."

The man answered him by levelling a pistol at his head; but, when he pulled the trigger, the powder did not even flash in the pan.

"You see," continued Antonio, "that pistol is my servant also. Begone, then, lest you lie there with your master."

He pointed impatiently to the door, whereto the man slunk in awe, muttering "'La Force' is dead." They heard him a moment later galloping wildly through the woods with the same cry upon his lips.

"Mademoiselle," said Antonio, very quietly, "it

is fortunate that I took the opportunity to spill my wine upon the pan of yon fellow's pistol while we sat at supper, or assuredly he would have blown my brains out. Now, if it be agreeable to you, we will bind up this rogue in his own table-cloth and carry him to Paris with us as a souvenir of this evening."

"To Paris!" cried Corinne, in amazement, "and what shall we do with him in Paris, my dear Antonio?"

"We shall punish him for his audacity in stopping the coach of Corinne de Montesson. Did I not tell you that my mysteries were more powerful than the sword of your kinsman, Bénoît? Have patience a little while and you shall doubt my word no more."

Corinne could not repress a word of fear.

"You carry your jest far — it seems to me that the man is dead."

"Indeed, there is very little the matter with him, mademoiselle — so little that I fear to hear him tell us so if we delay. Run back to the coach, then, and bid one of the men attend me. If the third knave should desire to know what we have done to his master, ask him to come to the house and I will show him."

She did not answer him, but, drawing her cloak about her, ran off swiftly through the thicket.

THE MAN ANSWERED HIM BY LEVELLING A PISTOL.

STRANGE AFFAIR AT FONTENAY

When the lacqueys and the third of the robbers arrived at the chalet presently, they found "La Force" already bound hand and foot with the white cloth from his own table.

Indeed, a physician alone could have told that he lived; and when the remaining highwayman saw the body he reeled back as though a pistol had been fired in his face.

"Rascal!" cried Antonio, taking advantage of the situation to grip him by the throat and to clap a pistol to his head — one of the pistols he had snatched from the belt of "La Force" — "rascal! I have killed your master as you see, and am taking his body back to Paris as a warning to those who do not respect the name of my mistress. Choose, then, whether you will throw down your arms and have your liberty, or be taken to Paris to die upon the gibbet."

The man writhed and gasped under the powerful hand — but impotently — for the lacqueys had taken heart now and had made haste to seize him by the arms. When he spoke, it was to beseech the old physician to give him his liberty.

"By the God above me, we have trapped the devil this night!" said he; "show me but the back of a horse and you shall see my face no more, monsieur."

Two minutes later, he also was galloping through the woods, crying like one demented, "'La Force' is dead." But the body of his master lay secure upon the top of Corinne's coach, where, rolling and jolting like a log, it rested until the barrier was passed and the horses were driven through the gateway of the Hôtel Beautreilles. Dark as the night proved, many stopped in the narrow streets of the great city to point the finger at a burden so curious; many cried, "They carry a dead man, — what a thing to see!" But others only crossed themselves and lifted their hats. "She jests with the dead," they said, and hurried on, afraid.

It was one o'clock in the morning when "La Force," who had been conscious of a restless and troubled sleep, and of strange happenings in his dreams, wholly recovered his senses and sat up in the bed upon which unknown hands had laid him. He thought at the instant of waking that he had slept out in the woods by Gros Bois again; but when he rubbed his eyes and looked well around him, some of the events of the night began to shape themselves again in his brain, and to be acted anew, until he remembered all things — even to the silver bowl and the horrible draught of vapour he had drunk therefrom.

"*Mort Dieu!*" said he, springing from his bed angrily, "it was the devil's bowl I drank from — a curse upon them! And now — and now — ?"

STRANGE AFFAIR AT FONTENAY

He began to examine the room with questioning eyes, but his curiosity was soon satisfied. It was a small apartment with walls of stone, in shape, a horseshoe; having for furniture a stool and a table, in addition to the plain wooden bed whereupon he had slept. Its only ornament was a crucifix hung high upon the crown of the apse.

"La Force" saw that the door was sheathed with iron and monstrous thick, like the door of a dungeon. A little window, heavily barred, permitted him, when he stood upon the tips of his toes, to see the world without. At the moment, however, such a privilege was worth little, for the night was moonless, and his keen eyes could detect nothing beyond a great black shape, which had no meaning to him. None the less did he begin to be haunted by the thought that he was in a prison; and when he had reflected a little while, he said it would be the prison of the Conciergerie.

This thought was slow to be accepted, slow to force itself upon his mind. He found himself at first laughing at the idea as a folly; but he could pause in his laughter to feel the damp sweat upon his brow and to sink upon the bed shivering with fear. Well he knew that, if his surmise were true, he might ask nothing more of life. They would send him to the galleys — possibly to death. He remembered the dashing life of the road, the women he had kissed, the gay company he had enjoyed, the debauches which had been kept in the house of the Silver Birch; and these pleasant memories helped him to stave off the dreadful omens of the cell. "God!" he said, "it cannot be that I shall never see the woods again!"

It needed a great effort to banish a sense of peril such as this; but he refused to hear the damning voices which haunted him; and anon, he got into bed again and tried to sleep. He was very weak after the trial of the night; and when he lay down and pulled the heavy covering over his head to shut out the light of the lantern which illumined the apartment, he found that he was hot as one in a fever, and that there was a new pain in his lungs which forbade him to rest.

Do what he would, recall as he might the most pleasant scenes of his past, a phantom figure ever at his side seemed to whisper, "You are come to the judgment." For a while he battled bravely with the spectre, but when a clock without struck two, he was able to endure the vision no longer, and he sprang from his bed in an agony of fear and of foreboding.

"Jesus!" he said, "it is my dream; that which I see is a thing of sleep. The sun will shine in my eyes presently, and I shall behold the forest again. My horse will come to me, and we will —"

A shadow falling across the floor cut short his pleasant promises. It was a dreadful shadow, magnified by the lantern's feeble light until it represented nothing human, being a horrid shape, eyeless, with masked face, and a head upon which a cap like a fool's cap was placed. "La Force" staggered against the bed when he beheld it, and covered his eyes with his hand.

"Mother of God!" he sobbed, "what do I see?"

"Monsieur," was the answer, in a low and gentle voice, "fear nothing from me. I come to warn you."

"La Force" turned his head and looked. A figure dressed in the rough black robe of a monk, but having the head and face covered with a pointed black hood, like the hood of the Misereri in Rome, stood motionless at his side. For a moment the highwayman succumbed to an overwhelming panic. He shrieked aloud at the terrible aspect of the phantom, believing that the devil stood with him in the cell.

"Oh, for pity's sake," he wailed, "tell me what this means."

"My son," said the monk, "it means that you have stopped the coach of Mademoiselle de Montesson; for which crime you now find yourself a prisoner in her house, where — "

He paused, as though he did not wish to finish the sentence; but the robber, being assured now that the apparition was no ghostly one, could not suppress his curiosity.

"Yes — yes," he asked eagerly, "where — ?"

"Where you are to die at dawn," said the monk.

"La Force" wiped the sweat from his brow and laughed like an hysterical woman.

"Bah," he said, "she will not kill me."

"My son," said the monk, very earnestly, "she will think no more of killing you than of crushing an insect in her path. Do you hear those blows? They are the blows of the axes which hew a scaffold for you. If you doubt me, look from yon window and you shall see — "

"La Force" ran to the window, and standing upon the tips of his toes looked into the court. Where darkness had prevailed ten minutes before, light — the light of fifty torches — now mastered the night. The highwayman saw that these torches were held by men gowned as his mysterious visitor, all in deep black, with hoods covering their faces, and holes for their eyes, which gave them an ogreish aspect terrible to behold.

But that which interested him more than all was the great structure they were helping to build — a structure of wood heavily draped in black.

STRANGE AFFAIR AT FONTENAY

Very familiar to him was that warning shape — the great cross-beam, the heavy side supports, the platform for the victim. He could even see a coil of rope curled like a snake upon the black carpet.

"Jesus!" he said, dropping upon his feet again, "they build a scaffold."

"Exactly," said the monk, "and at dawn they will have finished their work."

"La Force" felt his heart beating quickly, but he nerved himself to look out of the window again.

"Holy God, have pity upon me; I see a coffin!" he exclaimed, reeling back from the casement and falling, terror-struck, upon the bed. "Oh, monsieur, of your charity beseech a little mercy for me. I cannot die — I have sin upon my soul."

The monk watched his agony unmoved.

"My son," said he, "of that which we sow assuredly we must reap. Forget not that your harvest is death. At dawn you will garner the fruit you have fostered so well. Remember that the sun will shine down to-morrow, not upon your eyes glad to behold the day again, but upon the earth which lies heavy upon a spiritless body. Think of that, and be warned, for here mercy is unknown."

"La Force" answered him with a great oath and a threat, lifting his clenched hand to strike the speaker; but the monk seized the upraised arm by the wrist and threw the robber to the ground with such force that he lay there many minutes stunned and bruised. When he looked up again the monk had left the cell.

He heard a clock strike three at this time; but the sound of hammering still continued in the court without, and although he dared not to look again, he made sure that the scaffold must be now near its completion.

Had it been given him to die upon the highroad in some affair where swords clashed and pistols made merry music, he would have shown a bold face enough; but to be killed like a rat in a trap, to swing like a common thief, simply because he had compelled a woman to sup with him against her will, was a punishment not to be borne.

There were moments when he raved like a madman, beating with his fists against the cold stone wall, or casting himself in rabid fits of fury at the iron-sheathed door. At other moments he lay upon his bed in a stupor, scarcely seeming to breathe, trying in his mind to imagine that the end was passed, and that he lay in his coffin, still and voiceless, beneath a heavy weight of earth. When at length a glimmer of day struck the dark court without, and came with timid step even into his cell, he had no longer the mind either to fear or hope. A dull and merciful insensibility to thought prevailed.

It was half-past five precisely when the door of his cell was opened, and the monk, accompanied by three others similarly habited, re-entered the prison and bade "La Force" arise.

"Monsieur," said the monk, "the hour has come. Have courage, then, and drink a cup of wine. Remember what a reputation you bear, and do not let them speak of you as other than the brave man I know you to be."

"La Force" opened his eyes, for he was half asleep.

"Christ!" said he, "I dreamed that I was in the woods again."

He was like a man walking in a sleep now; and he drank off the wine they offered him, protesting that he was ready to die; but no sooner were the words spoken, than he fell into an uncontrollable fit of sobbing, and, throwing himself upon his knees, he craved mercy of them. The four hooded men gave no sign that they heard him, but stood like messengers of death, silent and unmoved. Nor did they speak when they led him from the cell presently, and, coming out into the court, he beheld a towering scaffold with a masked executioner upon the steps of it, and other hooded men ready to assist in the last great act.

"La Force" had never thought that death could wear a shape so awful. The cold light of dawn, the silent, hooded figures, the gaunt black scaffold, struck his heart with a deadly and overwhelming fear. He gave one long-drawn cry of agony, and then fell fainting upon the stone floor.

But at the moment when he fell, a great shout of laughter went up in the court, and one of the monks, pulling aside his hood, exclaimed: "Haste to drive him to Gros Bois. The drug that was in the wine acts for three hours. Let him be quite alone when he awakes."

"La Force" awoke when the church bells in the village of Gros Bois were proclaiming the Angelus. They had laid him in the heart of a solitary thicket, wherefrom, through a bower of the trees, he could espy a little pond shining like a silver mirror in the generous sunshine. But he was very weak when the spell of the drug passed, and he lay for long minutes content to feel the sweet morning air blowing upon his face, and to gaze up at the cloudless heaven above him.

"Holy Virgin," he said, "can it be that I live —that I have dreamed the things of the night! Is it I, 'La Force,' who speaks, or do I hear voices in the grave? Oh, Heaven pity me, for I have suffered."

Slowly and with painful effort he dragged himself to the pond. A horse whinnied in a neighbouring brake as he went, and he knew that it was his own horse calling to him.

"Oh," he said, "how good it is to live — how good! Last night I died ten deaths, but to-day — to-day —"

He tried to collect his thoughts and to knit the story of this night together, but confused images played with his brain, and he could recall nothing. Once or twice the old fear came back to him. His heart quickened when he remembered the masked men and the heavy blows of those who had hewn out his scaffold. But this mood passed, and at length he crawled to the pond and began to lap up the water.

A tree shaded the place where he lay, and the water being clear and without a ripple, he beheld his own image reflected in it; and at this he started back from the bank, and his trembling hands clutched the grass convulsively.

"God!" he said, "she was right — she *is* a dangerous guest."

YERUT THE DWARF

VIII

YERUT THE DWARF

CHAMILLART, MARQUIS DE LA SUZE, entered the garden of the Hôtel Beautreillis when the clocks of Paris were striking five. He was dressed with scrupulous care, but the heavy coat of black satin with the ample skirts, dictated by fashion in the year 1766 — the heavy coat, and the full wig which fell upon his stooping shoulders, were allies of the summer heat. Chamillart, Marquis de la Suze, also Grand Marshal of the palace, used his handkerchief very freely, and declared that the weather was atrociously warm. And this was an observation not to be contested.

There was no one in the garden — an old garden umbrageously sweet and alive with the vesper note of birds — when the lacquey led so distinguished a visitor to a little bower of chestnut-trees, girt about with roses in full bloom, and carpeted with ripe grass and the petals of the flowers of yesterday. Here was a couch of ivory and satin and a little table, upon which a golden flagon of wine was set, and cups beside it, and fruit to cool the lips. Chamillart, Marquis de la Suze, bade the lacquey tell his mistress that his business was urgent. Then he filled a cup of wine and drank it at a draught. Certainly, the day was atrociously hot.

Had it been anywhere else than the Hôtel Beautreillis in the Rue St. Paul, had the mistress of the house been any one but pretty Corinne, with whom all Paris was properly in love, the Grand Marshal would have swollen visibly before the eyes of that lacquey who had asked him to cool his heels in a garden; but since it *was* the Hôtel Beautreillis, and Corinne *was* unquestionably mistress of it, he contented himself with a prodigious pinch of snuff and many impatient shufflings of the feet, and an attempt to stoop and pick a trailing rose; but there nature hindered him, for he was very stout, — without doubt it was a hot day.

Corinne de Montesson came tripping out of the house like a schoolgirl from a convent. She was dressed in that costume known as the *négligé apparent* — a girlish dress, suggesting shepherdesses and Elysian fields, and masquerade at Trianon. A straw hat half concealed the wealth of pretty silken hair which fell upon her shoulders, and was rebelliously untrammelled about her little ears. Her arms and neck were bare, and white as the marble of the fountains. She carried a volume of

Racine in her hand; a merry laugh rippled upon her lips.

Chamillart, Marquis de la Suze, leaned heavily upon his gold-mounted cane, and watched the pretty picture.

"*Ventrebleu!*" he said to himself, "she cannot be twenty-five years old — I do not believe it; she is eighteen, fifteen — she is an angel, and I am going to make her cry."

It may have been that, among the other reflections of this wicked old fop, there was one which told him how pleasant it would be to wipe away the tears of Corinne de Montesson. But that he concealed when he rose to salute her. Indeed, following the extravagant habit of the times, he stood bowing for quite a long time; and while he did so, he covered his heart with his three-cornered hat, as though in heart and hat lay all the emotions which had prompted his visit.

"*Chère* Corinne, you have no pity, you make me wait, — me, Chamillart — the minutes are hours — I grow old in this garden — "

She laughed coquettishly, for the day was rare when Chamillart, Marquis de la Suze, did not amuse her very much.

"Oh, monsieur, it is really too hot for compliments," she said, sinking into a low chair placed by the side of his couch. "Am I not grateful to any one who comes to the Hôtel Beautreillis on such a day? Let me give you some wine, and you shall repay me with all the news."

The Grand Marshal put down his hat very carefully, and then took up that position upon the sofa whence he could look with least effort into the pretty eyes of his hostess.

"The news!" he said, "oh, as for that, there is no news. Madame de Bouffleurs is not in Paris."

"She is at Yères, then?"

"Nowhere else. She left yesterday with two coaches, seven lacqueys, and a letter full of scolding from her kinsman, the Bishop of Bruges. She has gone to keep a retreat, and the Chevalier Leduc will follow her to-morrow. But, of course, we do not know that he is going to Yères."

The Grand Marshal chuckled horribly. Corinne was amused.

"If Madame de Bouffleurs has gone to Yères," she cried, "we shall have a holiday indeed. It will be Lent again, my dear marquis. There will be no scandals, and think of it, no unhappy lovers. How will Paris live for a week when that wicked tongue is still?"

"Impossible, my child. As impossible as the happiness of Chamillart, without the words of Corinne de Montesson."

"A compliment, a compliment! Is not that forbidden, Monsieur le Marquis?"

"Mademoiselle, beauty is as far above the law as the stars above the darkness."

He covered his heart with his hand again, and said to himself, —

"It is a pity that she must cry presently."

But Corinne knew nothing of his thoughts. She was telling herself that the visit of this doddering old man, whose gallant antics had amused her so often, was a misfortune of an already troublesome day. How long was he going to stop? Why was he at the Hôtel Beautreillis at all?

"You come from the palace, monsieur?" she asked, when the Grand Marshal had ceased for a moment to ogle her.

"From the palace, mademoiselle."

"And of whom were they talking?"

"Of the Count of Brives, *chère* Corinne."

Corinne's face flushed crimson. The Grand Marshal turned away his head.

"I would give half my riches if she would flush for me like that," he thought.

"And what did they say of the Count of Brives?" asked Corinne, making a violent effort to conceal her emotion.

"They were very sorry for him, mademoiselle."

"Sorry, monsieur, for Eugène — that is, for Monsieur le Comte?"

"Certainly, my child; but have you not heard the news?"

"Did you not tell me there was no news?"

"Yes; but how should I know that this would be news — to Corinne de Montesson?"

"Oh, for pity's sake, tell me!" she exclaimed, rising and stamping with a pretty gesture of impatience. "Tell me, Monsieur le Marquis, what are they saying of Eugène Sabatier?"

The Grand Marshal shrugged his shoulders.

"She is going to cry," he thought, "and I forgot to bring a second lace handkerchief." But Corinne persisted.

"Mademoiselle," he said at last, "I thought you would have known. Madame has prevailed with the king, and the Count of Brives will be in the Bastille to-morrow."

A cry escaped her lips; Corinne's cheeks were rosy no more. She stood, white as marble; a blow would not have hurt her more than the tidings which the Grand Marshal carried.

"Oh, it cannot be! it cannot be!" she cried. "Eugène — the Bastille — oh, I will not believe it! — what crime has he committed — whom has he wronged — is he not the king's friend, monsieur?"

"Without doubt, all that is true, my child; but

there are other friends, and they are more powerful. It has been the misfortune of Monsieur le Comte to offend one of those friends. He who puts honesty against a pretty face fights a losing battle, Corinne. When that pretty face has for its neighbour the ear of a king, poor honesty is already worsted. Your friend the count is young, or he would know that the compliments we pay a woman are the apologies for the slander we shall put about when that woman's back is turned. He is also very foolish to be so many months at the palace without finding a word of flattery for its mistress."

He chuckled, for he was grown old in the practice of polished mendacities. But Corinne was thinking — her quick brain was already at work; one idea possessed her — she must save Eugène Sabatier.

"Tell me," she cried with sudden impatience, "did the king wish this, monsieur?" And then, without waiting for his answer, —

"Oh, I do not believe it; the king is his friend; if Eugène could speak for himself, it would never be. They have told lies about him; it is the work of Madame du Barry — she has hated him from the first; it is her triumph, but it will not last — I shall prevent it, Monsieur le Marquis, I, Corinne de Montesson — "

Her face was crimson again, but it was with

excitement. Old Chamillart watched her with chuckling admiration. His little eyes danced; he leered and ogled like some old man of the sea who found himself, clothed in satin and jewels and fine lace, in some welcome garden of delights.

"*Ma foi*," he cried enthusiastically, "who would not have such a deliverer! Of course you will save him. It is for that I am come here. You will begin work now — to-day, this instant."

She stared at him with a new surprise, but began to listen intently.

"Hark to this," continued the Grand Marshal, with new gravity, "the Count of Brives is now at his château by the Weeping Rock of Ussy. If he could be warned to-day, to-night — if he could be warned by one who would tell him to ride for his life to the palace and there to see the king without a moment's delay, the letter which Villefort, the Captain of the Gendarmerie, now carries to Ussy, might yet be powerless to harm him —"

"They have sent Villefort, then!" exclaimed Corinne.

"He left Paris at four o'clock; he carries the king's warrant for the arrest of Eugène Sabatier; he will arrive at Ussy at midnight. After that hour, *chère* Corinne, no one in all France can save Monsieur le Comte from the woman he has insulted, and whose hour of vengeance has come.

But you will act before then — you will be on the road before the clock strikes again — you will find a plan. *Ma foi*, it will be a strange day when Corinne de Montesson, the cleverest woman in Paris, is outwitted by Villefort, the buffoon of the guard, the lumberer, the ape! But she will not be outwitted; to-morrow I shall hear a good story. It will be the story of the confusion of Captain Villefort — "

But Corinne was listening to him no longer. The great silver gong at her side already gave out its mellow note warningly; Bénoît, her kinsman, the first swordsman in Paris, came hurrying to her side.

"Where is Yerut?" she asked, utterly unable to suppress her excitement. "Send Yerut to me, and then let them bring horses. We ride to Ussy before the sun sets."

"Bravo! bravo!" cried the Grand Marshal, as he rose to go. "It is my own Corinne after all; to-morrow all Paris shall laugh at the Captain of the Guard and his twenty men — "

"You said twenty, monsieur?"

"No more, no less; twenty and one against the prettiest wits in Paris. It is good to have the friendship of those pretty wits, *chère* Corinne — but, blood of Paul, who comes here?"

He started, clutching his cane convulsively, for

there came of a sudden to the bower a figure so strange that nothing like to it had been seen by any one in Paris. It was the figure of Yerut, the dwarf. Hideous, stunted, with hair shaggy as the fur of a bear, with hands like claws, with deep-set shining eyes, agile and quick, ready to leap or dance — Corinne de Montesson had no more faithful servant in all her great house than Yerut. And now she knew that the life of her lover depended upon the sagacity and the fidelity of this poor creature.

"Yerut," she said, "you know Villefort, the Captain of the Guard?"

A grunt of assent seemed to come from the heart of the dwarf.

"He has ridden from Paris to arrest the Count of Brives. He will pass the Weeping Rock before midnight. You must overtake him at the Inn of Ussy and detain him there until we come. Take the swiftest Arab we have — you understand?"

Yerut bowed low. He vanished from the garden like an arrow from a bow.

"To horse! to horse!" cried Corinne, clapping her hands impatiently. "There is not an instant to lose."

But old Chamillart hobbled away to his coach with a heavy heart.

"I should have postponed the day of my birth

for thirty years," he said to himself. "Certainly, she will never cry 'to horse' for me."

And that was another observation not to be contested.

. . . .

The great clock in the tower of the monastery of Franchard struck eleven when Villefort, the Captain of the King's Guard, found himself at the foot of the Roche qui Pleure. He could hear the strange note of that watery bell, melodious as the sound of weird music, in the silence of the vast forest of Fontainebleau. Winter or summer, drought or flood, the great rock would shed its silver tear musically into the pearly shell below it. Guides listened for the splash of the water, and went on gladly because of it; peasants worshipped before the heavenly well, and quenched their thirst at the pure fount of miracles. But to Villefort it was no more than the signal that his work was almost accomplished; that when another hour had passed he would lay his hands upon the traitor, Eugène Sabatier.

He rode slowly, his twenty men following with heavy eyes and hard words for a task which brought them to the forest when they should have been in their comfortable beds in Paris. The glory of the hour was nothing to Henri de Villefort. The enchanting light which fell upon the mighty thickets, the moonbeams playing upon the rippling lake, the lengthening shadows, with all their suggestion of elves and spirits, had no enchantment for him. For Henri de Villefort was afraid — afraid of the dark places of the wood, afraid of the silence, afraid of the hag's tales which his men had not failed to recite to him during their ride from the Barrière d'Enfer.

"Bah!" he had said, spurring his horse in anger. "Who would believe such things, at this time of day? I shall follow the great road to Ussy; there are twenty men with me. I care not a crown for all the devils in the legends. Saint John be my witness, I fear no living man."

The trooper addressed shrugged his shoulders disdainfully.

"They do not live, captain," he said gloomily. "They are the dead who died a thousand years ago; they breathe upon you cold breath, and your skin dries up with fever. You go mad and leave your bones for them to lie upon. I heard it at Franchard when I was a singing boy there. God bring us all back to Paris again, is my word."

Villefort swore a big oath, and rode on in silence. He did not speak again until the music of the Weeping Rock was a melodious echo, but thereafter he began to learn that it was no great highway which led to the Château of Ussy. Through dreadful copse and darkened brake, by paths overhung with trailing creeper and thorny bramble, in the gloom of mighty oaks and spreading chestnuts, — so must this hostile pilgrimage be made. The glory of the moonbeams, sparkling upon the dewy grass, did but light up weirdly the tangled heart of the deeper forest. The fireflies glowing in the woods were for him the evil eyes of the elves he could not see. The nightingale sang warningly. It was as though unseen enemies peopled the groves about him. He thought every minute to feel the touch of a hand upon his shoulder.

And this was his state of mind when a dreadful cry, like the cry of a soul in agony, came without warning out of the thicket upon his left hand and seemed to freeze the very blood of the twenty-one who rode to Ussy.

"Saints and angels, hark to that!" cried Villefort, drawing rein with trembling hands.

Again the cry arose — again and again. The troopers sat still as statues in the moonlight. Villefort could hear his heart beating; the fiend himself, he thought, was at his elbow.

"Pish!" he said presently, though the words seemed to choke him, "it is a wolf at supper, and that is the cry of the dish. Are we all women, to draw rein at shadows?"

"Not at all, Monsieur de Villefort, not at all,"

answered a voice from the thicket whence the cry came; "I will stake my life that there is not a woman among you, or if there be, why then she wears a better face than the Captain of the King's Guard."

A deep laugh, like the boom of a merry bell, followed the words. The guards were still listening to it when, with a great snapping of twigs and bursting of bramble, the speaker forced his horse from the covert and confronted Monsieur de Villefort.

"Holy Michael, defend us from all devils this night!" groaned Villefort, while cold sweat stood upon his brow and his quaking hand closed nervously about the butt of his pistol.

Yerut, the dwarf, for it was he who had raised the cry and had answered the Captain of the Guard, was clothed from head to foot in scarlet. Great boots, which appeared to be almost as large as the wearer, dangled from his saddle-flaps nearly to the ground. He wore a three-cornered cap cocked on the side of his shaggy head, and rode an Arab horse which still champed at his bit, though spurred from Paris to the Weeping Rock. Never did a stranger apparition confront man.

"Amen to your prayer, Monsieur de Villefort," cried the dwarf, gaily, — "amen and amen. The holy saints save us from all devils, and give us the light of their lamps to follow the road to Ussy."

"You go to Ussy, monsieur?" asked Villefort, taking heart a little when he saw the diamonds glistening upon the hilt of the stranger's sword. At the same time he said to himself, "Here is a brother of all the fiends."

The dwarf did not answer the question put so directly to him, but fell instead into a fit of uncontrollable laughter. The very woods rang with his merriment; he reeled in his saddle until his forehead touched the mane of his horse.

"Ho, ho, ho, ho!" he laughed, "how you amuse me, Monsieur de Villefort!"

"Amuse *you*," exclaimed Villefort, losing his temper; "who the devil are *you* that you should be amused?"

"A cat may laugh at a king, monsieur, and I am the cat. Is it not good to laugh? If it come to that, I have as good a reason to laugh as the Captain of the King's Guard to cry."

"As good a reason — ?" gasped Villefort.

"Certainly, since I go to Ussy to bury its master."

Villefort reined in his horse with a gesture as much of surprise as of will.

"To bury its master, monsieur!" he stammered, "but he is not dead. How can you bury a man who is not dead?"

The dwarf burst again into a merry fit of laughter.

"Ho, ho, ho, ho!" he roared, "what a dull fellow you are, Monsieur de Villefort! It is lucky for you that we met this night."

"Lucky?" exclaimed Villefort.

"As I say, lucky. For what is luck but gain, monsieur, and what is gain but happiness, and what is happiness but laughter, and what is laughter but wine, — which, by my faith, carries us back *ex argumento* to this, that wine is luck, and that Monsieur de Villefort of the King's Guard is a fool."

Villefort spluttered with rage; the dwarf touched his Arab lightly with his spurs, and began to hum the popular ballad, — *Voilà la taverne à la mode.*

"Name of the devil!" said Villefort, when he had found his tongue, "I have the mind to write my answer upon your back, *coquin* — "

The dwarf turned in his saddle, and showed a face so horrible that the Captain of the Guard felt his blood run cold. It was like the face of a Barbary ape. Villefort crossed himself instinctively; he prayed to all the saints to bring him quickly out of the cursed wood.

"Monsieur," snarled the dwarf, chattering horribly, "he who writes upon the back of Yerut the singer will read his own epitaph."

Villefort shuddered; the twenty behind him rode with white faces and prayers upon the bloodless lips.

YERUT THE DWARF

"Yerut the singer," said the Captain of the Guard, in a very humble voice; "you sing then, monsieur?"

"Like Lucifer himself," answered the dwarf; and then he fell into a strange, weird chaunt in a voice so harsh and grating that the very leaves of the thicket seemed to tremble —

>"De tous les corps de métiers,
>   Voilà ce fléau redoutable."

"Sing!" he continued, breaking off suddenly; "have I not the charm of Levasseur and the style of Legros? Do you not admit that, Monsieur de Villefort?"

"Certainly he is mad," muttered Villefort, in a low voice, but not so low that the dwarf did not hear him.

"Mad," he repeated, "ay, surely, as mad as Monsieur de Villefort, who goes to Ussy and blows a horn to tell all that he is coming."

"A horn, — I blow no horn," cried de Villefort.

"Let us not chop words. And I will tell you this, monsieur, that if you think to arrest the Count of Brives you are a fool for your pains."

"Pah!" said Villefort, "I ride with one of his friends."

"With so good a friend that at dawn I shall sing a requiem for him."

Villefort pricked up his ears.

"How can that be?" he asked.

"*Ma foi*," answered the dwarf, "it is no good asking you riddles, my captain. A wench at a book would be quicker. Do you not see that if I am to sing a requiem for the Count of Brives at dawn, some one must kill him to-night?"

"Ho, ho!" cried Villefort, "it is a duel, then?"

"Exactly, a duel."

"He goes out with you, monsieur?"

"With me? — pah, I do not kill men with swords."

Villefort bit his lip. His head was clearer now, and fear of the forest possessed him no longer. They had passed from the darkness of the wood by this time, and the lights of an inn shone through the vista of the trees. The Captain of the Guard was perplexed. He did not know what to make of the dwarf or of his story.

"Come," he said after a pause, "there will be no duel to-night; I shall prevent it."

"*You!*" replied the dwarf, who did not attempt to conceal his contempt. "*You* will prevent it, Monsieur de Villefort!"

"Certainly; I shall arrest the Count of Brives."

The dwarf roared with laughter.

"Ho, ho, ho, ho!" he laughed; "we will kiss the sun, we will walk with the moon, we will put the stars in our pockets."

Villefort ground his teeth.

"You think that I cannot arrest him?" he snarled.

"Think? I think nothing, monsieur; it is for the count to say. Were there no eyes in yon wood when we rode through? Were there none to cry, 'Here comes the fat Villefort to arrest our master'? — none to gallop to Ussy and give news of you? Body of Paul! if you think that you came unheralded to the château, you have not the wits of a German mountebank."

Villefort swore lustily.

"I never thought of that," said he. "You mean that he has been warned of my coming?"

"What else could I mean?"

"Then I have ridden upon a fool's errand."

"Could you ride upon any other, Monsieur de Villefort? I beg you, if you can employ those great ears of yours, to listen to that music. It is a horn winded in the park of the Château of Ussy. What think you now of your journey?"

The clarion note of a horn rang out musically in the stillness of the night. It echoed from copse to copse, and thicket to thicket, as though phantom horsemen hunted in the purlieus of the forest.

"Thousands devils!" exclaimed Villefort, "I am too late."

"There is no doubt of that, my dear captain. And being too late, you will do well to draw rein awhile at yonder tavern, where I shall introduce you presently to the Count of Brives himself."

"The Count of Brives is coming *here?*"

"Unquestionably he is. He will come before the clock strikes again, to fight my master, who stands before the door there. Meanwhile let me present you to the Chevalier Guibert."

They rode up to the tavern door with a great clatter of spur and caparison. Villefort, on his part, did not know whether he stood on his head or his heels; he was saying to himself that the Count of Brives had escaped him after all. While he did not believe the dwarf's story, and was still determined to search the château, he had the wish, nevertheless, to hear what the stranger might say, and to delay for that purpose while the host of the *auberge* could water the horses of his men and bring cups of wine. The troopers, glad in their turn to leave the darkness of the wood behind them, dismounted joyously, and were soon swarming in the little courtyard, to the great delight of the wenches of the inn, and the great confusion of its master.

There were two horsemen before the door of the *auberge;* one a big fellow dressed in black velvet, the other possessing a figure so fragile and so pretty, so slim and boyish, that passers-by might well have called it the figure of a girl. A group of servants, heavily armed and mounted on magnificent bay horses, stood apart, awaiting the pleasures of the travellers, the younger of whom was dressed in a suit of purple silk, and carried a sword in a scabbard frosted with diamonds of exceeding brilliancy. It was to the latter that Yerut the dwarf now presented Monsieur de Villefort.

"My master, the Chevalier Guibert — the Chevalier Guibert, my servant," he said, with a gesture of self-importance not to be described.

"Your servant!" roared Villefort. "Body of Paul, I have the mind to write that upon your tongue!"

The dwarf grinned horribly.

"You could not spell it, Monsieur de Villefort," said he.

Corinne, for she it was who wore the purple dress, silenced Yerut with a look.

"Monsieur," she said very sweetly, "you must forgive one who, though young in years, is old in liberties. That will be easier to do, since I am able to be of some service to you to-night."

"To be of service to me, monsieur?"

"As I say, to be of service to you. Have you not come to Ussy to arrest Eugène Sabatier?"

Villefort regarded the questioner closely.

"You know that, monsieur?"

"Undoubtedly, I know it; and since I alone can help you to succeed, you may not think it a waste of time to drink a cup of wine with me."

Villefort bowed stiffly, and entered the house with her. At the same moment, the dwarf was deep in talk with Gaspard, the rider in black, who had turned his horse towards the forest.

"We shall keep him an hour, if that be possible," said the dwarf. "The men will be drunk before then. Let the count ride for his life to Versailles; if time serve, he will find us at the cross-road beyond Essonne."

"The devil dry their throats!" muttered Bénoît, giving rein to his horse. "I count upon you, Yerut, in all things. Hold yon booty but an hour, and no woman in France shall keep Eugène Sabatier from the king."

The dwarf stood to watch the darkness of the forest enshroud the galloping figure. Then he returned to the inn and found that Villefort and the Chevalier Guibert, his mistress, were already busy over a flask of wine, set out in a little room upon the first floor. But while the mock chevalier was comfortable in a low wooden chair, the Captain of the Guard paced the room as one who delays but an instant, and that unwillingly.

"Chevalier," he was saying, "it may be true that the Count of Brives is warned of my coming; yet if that be so, what madness will carry him to this inn when he should be upon the road to the frontier?"

"The same madness which makes the lark sing at dawn and the sun set at eve, monsieur," chimed in the dwarf, who squatted upon the table and raised a flagon merrily; "the madness of the cow for the moon; the howl of the dog when the horn is winded — the folly of Monsieur de Villefort who chases the stag — *ma foi*, the quest of a wench's pretty lips, and hey, for her eyes in the dark."

Villefort stopped in his walk. The flickering light of spluttering candles fell upon his angry face weirdly.

"Heaven deliver me from this madman!" he cried.

"Monsieur," said the dwarf, "it is the duty of fools to be sane. Would you have me dull my wits until they were no brighter than those of Henri de Villefort? And there you fall upon a plain tale, and shall see how truly I am mad. For if Nature teaches the lark to call for his mate, and sheds the dew upon the thirsty ground, shall she less befriend the man who, learning that the wench is at the inn, has the mind to sample the lips of yesterday! God's truth, my captain, it is writ as large as the nose on your ugly face."

Villefort raised his fist as though to strike the dwarf, but Corinne stood between them.

"Hold your tongue, Yerut," she said. "Indeed, monsieur, I know not how to excuse him, unless it be that with it all he tells you the truth. The Count of Brives would go a hundred miles to avoid this inn if he knew that the Chevalier Guibert awaited him here; but he would ride a hundred miles to reach it if one told him that Corinne de Montesson was to make it a house of call."

Villefort forgot his anger.

"You mean to say that he will come here to-night to meet her?"

"As he thinks, monsieur. My servant has even now ridden to the château to tell him that you have turned back to Franchard, and that Corinne de Montesson is here with news which will save his life."

Villefort roared with laughter. The dwarf roared, too; so that the very rafters rang with their shouts.

"Ho, ho, ho!" laughed Henri de Villefort, "you

tell him that his mistress is here, and when he comes you will cut his throat. How you love him, Chevalier!"

"How I love him!" muttered Corinne; and she meant every word she said.

"How he loves him!" roared the dwarf, choking with laughter and with wine.

But Corinne's heart beat wildly. She was asking herself if the tale had, indeed, borne such good fruit. She looked at the clock and saw that they had been already twenty minutes in the inn. She said that Bénoît was at the château, now; they were saddling the horses, — oh, for an hour, for an hour yet to win her lover's liberty!

Villefort ceased to laugh and went to the window.

"Saint John!" said he, "if the Count of Brives rides towards the inn, I will even go a little way to meet him," and then he bawled to his troops: "ho, there, you sots! — do you hear me calling?"

The dwarf leaped from the table and put his grinning head beside that of the captain.

"Ho, there, you sots," he repeated; "another bottle apiece to the health of the Chevalier Guibert!"

The troopers, who had come out into the moonlight, went, shouting, back to the kitchen of the inn —

"Ho, there, another bottle apiece to the health of the Chevalier Guibert!"

Yerut pulled Monsieur de Villefort from the window and shut it. Corinne's heart seemed to stand still.

"Upon my word, Monsieur de Villefort," said the dwarf, "you are a very foolish man. Would you tell all Ussy that you lie here this night? For Heaven's sake, hold your tongue, or if you cannot do that, bury it in this flagon."

He pushed a flagon of wine toward the Captain of the Guard. Villefort did not notice the curious taste of the liquor; but when he had drunk, his head swam and the candles danced before his eyes.

"I shall go to Ussy," he cried doggedly. "It is a plot to detain me here."

The dwarf took a pack of cards from his pocket and began to cut it. Corinne looked at the clock. Would the great hand never reach the hour? It seemed so to her.

"Go or stay," cried Yerut, with indifference, "it is the same to me and to my master; and I will tell you this, captain, that if we did not wish to see the Count of Brives very much we would not rest another hour with so impertinent a fellow."

Villefort, who was dizzy with the drugged wine

Brought it with a Crash upon the Head of Henri de Villefort.

and enraged beyond endurance, drew his sword and confronted the dwarf.

"Dog!" he roared, "I will teach you manners. That is the tenth time you have insulted me this night."

"The eleventh, monsieur," said Yerut, who still squatted upon the table. "The eleventh, as I live; and you do well to count, for I am going to make it twelve."

Leaping up with a cat-like agility, the dwarf seized a flagon of wine and brought it crash upon the head of Henri de Villefort. So terrible was the blow, that the Captain of the Guard reeled back to the wall; and, while the liquor still poured down his gaudy vest and dripped from his lank hair, the drug they had given him did its work, and he fell senseless upon the sanded floor.

Two minutes later the Chevalier Guibert and Yerut the singer rode from the courtyard of the inn. To the troopers, gathered round them inquiringly, they said, —

"Another flask to the health of the Captain of the Guard!"

And so, throwing crowns upon the flags, they galloped from Ussy, and soon were lost to view in the labyrinth of the forest.

. . . .

Dawn, grey-garbed and melancholy, was hovering above the valley of the Seine when the Count of Brives and Bénoît, who rode with him, drew rein at the parting of the ways beyond Essonne. A mist of morning lay upon the awakening pastures; the rushes bent to the flood of the swirling waters; night answered reluctantly to the heralds of the lagging sun. Dew lay thick upon the brown-burnt grasses; the air was chill and searching as a breath of winter.

"They do not come," said Bénoît, whose horse, like that of the other, was white with foam. "God grant that Yerut has not failed us."

"I think of mademoiselle," said the count, impatiently. "What is it to me that I am upon the road to Versailles if misfortune has overtaken her at Ussy?"

"*Ma foi*, you complain too soon, count. Hark to that music; it is the ring of hoofs behind us!"

They listened a little while, and then were sure. The sounds magnified and became clearer; care passed from the boyish face of Eugène Sabatier.

"It is Corinne," he cried joyfully. "Oh, God be thanked!"

Two figures loomed up from the mists; two horses were reined back upon their haunches.

"Eugène, is it thou?"

"Corinne, beloved!"

But Yerut the dwarf was looking at the river,

and Bénoît, the kinsman of mademoiselle, became so blind of a sudden that he could scarce see the mane of his horse.

Henri de Villefort entered the gardens of Versailles at three o'clock of the afternoon. He still wore a coat upon which purple patches spoke of the inn at Ussy. His high boots were brown with the dust; his head was bandaged and his walk uncertain. Side by side with him walked Chamillart, Marquis de la Suze.

"You have failed, monsieur," exclaimed Chamillart, with assumed astonishment, "yet the Count of Brives was at his château last night."

Villefort ground his teeth.

"His friends surprised me," he stammered; "I crossed swords with one of them, and was wounded. There is fresh blood upon my coat now, and it was fifteen hours ago —"

He was about to continue his apologies when from a tree upon his right hand there came that haunting demoniacal cry he had heard in the forest of Fontainebleau when Yerut the singer had confronted him. It rose and fell like the wailing of the wind; it froze the words upon the lips of Henri de Villefort.

"Thousand devils!" he yelled, "it is the man monkey again —"

"At your service, Monsieur de Villefort — you seek the Count of Brives; he is yonder with the king, who has just given him a command."

The dwarf was perched upon the branch of the tree. His lap was full of sweetmeats; he grinned like a cat, but fell presently to laughing incontrollably, as he had laughed in the forest.

"Ho, ho, ho, ho! — you crossed swords with one of the count's friends, Monsieur de Villefort! Body of Paul, it was with the wine bottle that you fought — "

"You lie," retorted Villefort; "I fought with the Chevalier Guibert — "

"Who is yonder with the count? — but he wears a petticoat this morning, my captain. What a thing to tell in the palace that Henri de Villefort was worsted by a woman!"

"Dog!" roared Villefort, "it is to you that I owe this, to you and your lies — you who were to bury the master of Ussy — "

"*Tais-toi, tais-toi,*" answered the dwarf, "look at yon pair, and tell me if my mistress is not also master of Ussy, *cher* Monsieur de Villefort. But the Chevalier Guibert we buried last night. A truth, a truth! And now they laugh at you, captain. The king laughs. The queen laughs. I, Yerut, laugh."

Villefort could stand it no more. He strode

YERUT THE DWARF

away with the dwarf's horrid laughter still ringing in his ears; but old Chamillart, who watched Corinne and the count pacing the distant avenue by the side of Louis the Well-beloved, chuckled horribly.

"I said she would fool him," he muttered; "I said that she would save her lover — Saint John, if she would but look into my eyes like that!"

"Ho, ho!" said the dwarf in the tree, "she can look into the eyes of a wolf every day."

And then he fell to singing: —

"A quel diable ce drôle allait-il à l'école?"

Chamillart, Marquis de la Suze, shook his cane at the imp, and turned sadly from the garden.

THE END

www.ingramcontent.com/pod-product-compliance
Lightning Source LLC
Chambersburg PA
CBHW022056230426
43672CB00008B/1194